GUID

C000052167

Edited by **Rachel Tranter and Olivia Warburton**

15 The Chambers, Vineyard
Abingdon OX14 3FE
brf.org.uk

Bible Reading Fellowship is a charity (233280)
and company limited by guarantee (301324),
registered in England and Wales

ISBN 978 1 80039 178 9

This edition © Bible Reading Fellowship 2023
Cover image © Yotsuya/stock.adobe.com

Distributed in Australia by:
MediaCom Education Inc, PO Box 610, Unley, SA 5061
Tel: 1 800 811 311 | admin@mediacom.org.au

Distributed in New Zealand by:
Scripture Union Wholesale, PO Box 760, Wellington
Tel: 04 385 0421 | suwholesale@clear.net.nz

Acknowledgements

Notes by Andy Angel, Rosie Button, Stephen Finamore and Bill Goodman
commissioned by Helen Paynter.

A catalogue record for this book is available from the British Library

Printed by Gutenberg Press, Tarxien, Malta

Suggestions for using *Guidelines*

Set aside a regular time and place, if possible, when and where you can read and pray undisturbed. Before you begin, take time to be still and, if you find it helpful, use the BRF prayer on page 6.

In *Guidelines*, the introductory section provides context for the passages or themes to be studied, while the units of comment can be used daily, weekly or whatever best fits your timetable. You will need a Bible (more than one if you want to compare different translations) as Bible passages are not included. Please don't be tempted to skip the Bible reading because you know the passage well. We will have utterly failed if we don't bring our readers into engagement with the word of God. At the end of each week is a 'Guidelines' section, offering further thoughts about or practical application of what you have been studying.

Occasionally, you may read something in *Guidelines* that you find particularly challenging, even uncomfortable. This is inevitable in a series of notes which draws on a wide spectrum of contributors and doesn't believe in ducking difficult issues. Indeed, we believe that *Guidelines* readers much prefer thought-provoking material to a bland diet that only confirms what they already think.

If you do disagree with a contributor, you may find it helpful to go through these three steps. First, think about why you feel uncomfortable. Perhaps this is an idea that is new to you, or you are not happy about the way something has been expressed. Or there may be something more substantial – you may feel that the writer is guilty of sweeping generalisation, factual error, or theological or ethical misjudgement. Second, pray that God would use this disagreement to teach you more about his word and about yourself. Third, have a deeper read about the issue. There are further reading suggestions at the end of each writer's block of notes. And then, do feel free to write to the contributor or the editor of *Guidelines*. We welcome communication, by email, phone or letter, as it enables us to discover what has been useful, challenging or infuriating for our readers. We don't always promise to change things, but we will always listen and think about your ideas, complaints or suggestions. Thank you!

To send feedback, please email **enquiries@brf.org.uk**, phone **+44 (0)1865 319700** or write to the address shown opposite.

Writers in this issue

Bill Goodman encourages and enables lifelong learning in the Anglican diocese of Sheffield. *Yearning for You*, the published version of his PhD, is a conversation between the Psalms, Song of Songs and contemporary songs.

George M. Wieland lives in New Zealand, where he is the director of mission research and formation at Carey Baptist College, Auckland. Prior to that, he served in church and community ministry in England, Scotland and Brazil.

Andy Angel is the vicar of St Andrew's, Burgess Hill. Previously, he taught New Testament in two Anglican training colleges and his books include *Playing with Dragons* (Cascade, 2014) and *Intimate Jesus* (SPCK, 2017).

Rosie Button is a lecturer in New Testament and mission at All Nations Christian College. She has previously taught biblical studies and Greek in theological colleges in Zimbabwe and Uganda and at Redcliffe College.

Alison Lo is associate professor of Old Testament at Bethel Seminary. She has taught at the Chinese University of Hong Kong, London School of Theology, Moorlands Midlands Centre and Baptist Theological Seminary, Singapore.

Sally Nash is a theological educator, ministry consultant, spiritual accompanier, author and mentor (**sallynash.co.uk**). She is senior research fellow at St Padarn's Institute and associate minister at Hodge Hill Church, Birmingham.

Stephen Finamore is principal at Bristol Baptist College. Steve has worked as a pastor, as a lawyer and in community development in inner London and the Peruvian Andes.

Steve Walton is professor of New Testament at Trinity College, Bristol. He is a retired international volleyball referee and lives in Loughborough with his wife Ali, an Anglican minister and their Border Terrier, Flora.

Ashley Hibbard is a research associate at the Centre for the Study of Bible and Violence, and an adjunct lecturer at African Christian College, Eswatini and Emmanuel Bible College, Kitchener, Canada.

Michael Parsons was until recently the minister for discipleship at Lechlade Baptist Church. He has previously been a theology lecturer in the UK and Australia and commissioning editor for Paternoster and BRF.

Rosalee Velloso Ewell is a Brazilian theologian from São Paulo. She holds a PhD from Duke University, USA, and serves as director of church relations for the United Bible Societies. Rosalee lives with her family in Birmingham.

The editors write...

God's word is 'better to [us] than thousands of gold and silver pieces' (Psalm 119:72, NRSV). This issue of *Guidelines* gives treasure upon treasure as our contributors unpack God's word and lead us closer to him.

We're excited to start a new five-issue series by Bill Goodman, who will be taking us all the way through the Psalms, one book at a time. We also continue three series from the previous issue. Andy Angel continues taking us through Matthew 15—28, this time focusing on Jesus' various confrontations with religious leaders. Following on from Pauline Hoggarth's series on the oft-neglected minor prophets, Alison Lo looks at Joel, Obadiah, Micah and Zephaniah. Finally, Stephen Finamore brings us part three of his four-part study of Romans. We have 'unwrapped' Romans and 'run with' Romans; this time we are 'rolling with' Romans as we look at chapters 9—12.

We have some wide-ranging themes to explore too. George Wieland gives us a fascinating tour through intercultural Bible reading. His notes are written out of a research project where people from different cultural and ethnic backgrounds read and discuss the same Bible passage: groups of Māori, Samoan, Ni-Vanuatu, Fijian, Indian and Sri Lankan, Burmese, Chinese, Filipino and other readers. Sally Nash also brings us reflections on her PhD topic of shame and the church, looking at different types of shame and what the church can learn from these. Rosie Button brings us a reflection on refugees, which unfortunately is always a relevant topic.

Finally, we have excellent contributions from Steve Walton and Ashley Hibbard on Ruth and Deuteronomy respectively. And in the New Testament, Michael Parsons brings us detailed notes on 2 Peter, while Rosalee Velloso Ewell unpacks Philippians.

The Bible truly is a treasure chest full of gold and silver, and we hope that these reflections will help you further understand what a gift we have in this treasure.

Thank you to everyone who has taken the time to send in feedback since we took over as editors. We really appreciate receiving feedback, positive or negative, as it helps us to develop *Guidelines* further. If you have a comment, please share it by emailing **enquiries@brf.org.uk**, phoning **+44 (0)1865 319700** or writing to the address on page 2.

The BRF Prayer

Faithful God,
thank you for growing BRF
from small beginnings
into a worldwide family of ministries.
We rejoice as young and old
discover you through your word
and grow daily in faith and love.
Keep us humble in your service,
ambitious for your glory
and open to new opportunities.
For your name's sake,
Amen

Psalms Book I: David's prayers and teaching (Psalms 1—41)

Bill Goodman

Opening the book of Psalms, we soon notice its diversity. We find praises alongside laments, pleas for help and thanksgiving for salvation, accounts of Israel's history, celebrations of God's law, reflections on wisdom, homages to earthly kings and to the divine King.

Many commentators have recognised a few distinct groups within the Psalter, such as the 'Psalms of Korah' (Psalms 42—49) and the 'Songs of Ascents' (Psalms 120—134), but beyond that there is no clear organising principle. Recent studies, however, have reverted to the traditional framework of five sections or books of Psalms, each of which ends with a similar closing expression of praise (e.g. Psalm 41:13). In early times, the rabbis saw the Psalms as King David's gift to Israel of five books, just as Moses gave the first five books of scripture (Genesis to Deuteronomy). Here was 'Torah [instruction] of David', to stand alongside the 'Torah of Moses'. Over the next five issues of *Guidelines*, we shall explore a selection from each of these five 'books' of Psalms.

Some psalms present themselves as 'David's' (*le-Dawid* in Hebrew). This could mean 'by David', indicating that he was the writer; but it could equally mean 'to/for David' (addressed or offered to the king), 'about David' or 'on behalf of David'. And David could refer to any of the kings in the historical line of David. But the fact that David's name is linked to so many of the psalms seems significant (although some translations unhelpfully omit the superscription headings of individual psalms which mention David and historical events). It seems very likely that David wrote some of the psalms. In addition, those who compiled this book, probably during and after the exile in Babylon, looked back on David as a model to inspire God's people: a flawed and needy person, seeking God's favour and direction, learning how to praise and pray in good times and in times of trouble. The figure of David represents Israel, while also evoking experiences which are common to every human being – including us.

Bible quotations are taken from the NRSV, or occasionally are the author's own translation. 'Yhwh' is used throughout in place of 'the Lord'.

1 Overture

Psalms 1—2

Like an overture which briefly introduces us to melodies which will emerge more fully in the music that follows, Psalms 1 and 2 provide a two-part introduction to the whole Psalter. Psalm 1 proclaims the importance of Yhwh's *Torah* – God's instruction (sometimes translated as 'law'). Here and in the psalms that follow, figurative language conjures up in our imaginations an image – in this case, a flourishing tree. Following the divine teaching produces a life that is rooted, nourished, resilient, productive, attractive, blessed by Yhwh ('LORD' in many of our English translations). Psalm 1 also introduces two groups of people who will feature repeatedly: the righteous, those who choose to follow God's instruction, and the wicked, those who choose to reject it. Further vivid imagery depicts this latter way of life as being like chaff (1:4) – something dry, lacking nourishment, transient, unfruitful; a sad waste of a life.

That final phrase of Psalm 1 is opened out in Psalm 2, as it confronts 'the way of the wicked'. This is seen in the rebellion of the world's powerful rulers, who demand autonomy while raging and refusing to submit to God. Psalm 2 also introduces us to God's chosen king, whom Yhwh has 'anointed' – *meshiaḥ* in Hebrew, from which we derive our English word 'messiah'. Yhwh is king over all the nations, enthroned in heaven; Yhwh chooses to express that sovereignty from the temple on Jerusalem's Mount Zion, mediating divine rule through a chosen human king. But that earthly king faces major struggles against enemies, while also finding in God a refuge from those enemies – further themes which will recur in the psalms that follow. Some of the New Testament writers found in Psalm 2 a lens through which to see Jesus more clearly – particularly in the psalm's intriguing reference to this anointed king as God's 'son' (2:7, echoing 2 Samuel 7:14; taken up in Mark 1:11; Acts 13:33; Hebrews 1:5, etc.).

Psalm 2 closes as Psalm 1 began, with the distinctive word *ashrē*, which means 'happy' or 'fortunate'. Human beings are called to meditate on God's *Torah* and to submit to God's rule. This is the way of life which brings real life, true contentment to those who will embrace its delights and demands. For a fuller experience of these stirring melodies, keep listening in as the music develops.

2 The king's vulnerability – and security

Psalm 3

Psalm 2 ended proclaiming the happiness of all who take refuge in Yhwh. But what does that look like in practice? This next psalm gives us a glimpse of the challenges involved.

Psalm 2 also declared God's triumph through an anointed human king. Psalm 3 begins with a glimpse of Israel's greatest king, David: not triumphant, but a vulnerable fugitive! The opening heading (superscription) links this psalm with 'David, when he fled from his son Absalom', referring to a coup attempt described in 2 Samuel 15. The headings found in this and other psalms are omitted or downplayed in some English translations, as they are understood to be added after the psalm was written – whereas in the Hebrew Bible, they form verse 1. It may be that David himself wrote this psalm, expressing his anguish at his son's military rebellion; or that it was written later in different circumstances, but seen as a good illustration of what David must have been through. Either way, it was preserved because it was seen to be a helpful guide for future believers in their worship.

Enemies are 'many, many, many' (three times in the opening few lines): the sense of imminent threat seems initially overwhelming. But another word also appears three times: 'deliver' (sometimes translated 'save' or 'help'). In verse 2, we see faith is challenged as the enemies deny that God will help; in defiance of this, the speaker calls on Yhwh to save (v. 7) and declares that God is the one who does save (3:8). An image from ordinary life depicts people with heads bowed down, which can indicate that they are preoccupied, depressed, ashamed, humiliated or in fear and submission – but the head is then lifted up when that particular burden is lifted. This is the speaker's experience of relationship with Yhwh (3:3).

The psalm that follows this one shares similar ideas and words: calling on God to answer (v. 4; 4:1), concern for honour (v. 3; 4:2) despite the many who say discouraging things (v. 2; 4:5). Since both these psalms refer to sleep, they are traditionally prayed in the morning (v. 5) and the evening (4:8). They hold out hope that, even in times of turmoil, God's faithful ones can sleep securely and rise to face each new day with God.

3 The good life

A self-righteous, 'holier-than-thou' attitude is something many people find deeply unattractive. Is that kind of attitude found in psalms such as this one (see also Psalms 5, 17, 18:20–24)?

When the psalms praise people as 'righteous', they are admired not so much for being morally outstanding but more for their sense of helplessness, their dependence on God and their desire to learn God's ways. The enemies they struggle with include their own sinfulness (vv. 3–5; also 32:3–5; 38:18). Turning to Yhwh in prayer is one of their main characteristics. Those described as 'the wicked', by contrast, are at fault for their arrogance and self-sufficiency, which leave no room for humble dependence on God.

The heading of Psalm 7 indicates that David sang this psalm to Yhwh 'concerning Cush, a Benjaminite' (a name not mentioned anywhere else in the Bible), suggesting attack by a fellow Israelite. The psalm itself refers to pursuers and enemies (plural). Whatever the story behind it, the sense of threat is unmistakable: the enemies want to pounce and devour their victim like a hungry lion (v. 2). The speaker responds, not claiming to be perfect but simply protesting that they have done nothing to provoke or deserve this attack; it is unjust and must therefore be an affront to a just God (vv. 3–9).

There is hope when facing unjust oppression. Evil has a self-destructive dimension which can be its undoing: falling into a pit you have dug yourself (perhaps seeking to find water or to catch wild animals) is a suitable downfall which may prompt a wry smile from those threatened with violence (vv. 15–16; see also 9:15–16). Yet the speaker still feels the need to plead with God to intervene and take action (vv. 6, 10–13; see also 10:1–2).

Self-righteousness is an ugly, insidious attitude to be watched out for and repented of when found. But being committed to goodness and being passionate about right and wrong must still be our calling, rather than indifference. When we speak or sing this kind of psalm in worship, we appropriate it for ourselves, and it challenges us. That challenge is to live out true goodness and righteousness in our own lives, while also striving for justice for those who are denied it by human wickedness.

4 Greatness and power

Psalms 3—13 form a distinct group – with a surprise at the heart of it: the Psalter's first burst of praise. In striking contrast to the struggles and angst of the lament psalms which surround it, Psalm 8 conveys serenity and a sublime sense of wonder. Enemies and avengers do get a mention (v. 2), but their threats seem barely relevant, overwhelmed by a vision of the greatness of God and God's calling on human beings.

Yhwh is the majestic sovereign over all the world – a key fact emphasised by repetition of the psalm's opening and closing phrases (vv. 1, 9). In comparison to the greatness of this glorious God – and even with the vastness and wonder of the rest of God's creation – humanity seems totally insignificant. Yet despite this, humans have a special calling. In the high point of the poem (v. 4), humans are depicted in royal terms as those granted dominion over God's works (vv. 5–6), in words that remind us of Genesis 1:27–28. They are to express Yhwh's rule and attitudes. Yhwh exercises power by sharing it, empowering humans in this risky act of self-giving love; that is the model humanity is to follow in exercising the power entrusted to us.

To make sense of our human identity and vocation, we need to hold together the centre and the boundaries of this psalm. If we focus too much on God's greatness and sovereignty, we may become passive, even lazy – shrugging our shoulders, waiting for God to sort out all the messes we make. But if we focus too strongly on our own role and power, our dominion may turn into domination, oppressing and damaging the world while ignoring God's ultimate claim on us. Achieving a wise balance is essential, not least in responding to our current global climate crisis.

Psalm 8 is headed 'A Psalm of David' – as are all the psalms of lament which frame it, with their reminders of how humans often use power badly. The 'I' who speaks in Psalm 8 brings an unexpected counterpoint to all the suffering of Psalms 3—13 – yet this 'David' lives in that same world. Exercising power on God's behalf, in God's way, sometimes proves costly for David, and also for us. Yet inhabiting this privileged and painful calling evokes moments of awestruck praise.

5 Despair and hope, together

The Psalms express a huge spectrum of human experience and moods – sometimes a mixture of them in the same psalm. Psalm 13, one of many in this early part of the Psalter that lament and protest loudly about all that is wrong and call on God for help, seems to turn quite suddenly, in the final two verses, from anguish to confidence. How can such a mixture of moods coexist, in just a few verses?

The opening fourfold cry 'How long?' is passionate and poignant. This is not a request for information and a timeline, more a cry of intense frustration, a plea to end the suffering. Repetition increases the sense of desperation and impatience. The situation prompting these words about pain, sorrow and the enemy (v. 2) is unclear, giving them resonance with different aspects of our own lives. As readers, we can find these verses rousing our emotions, putting us in touch with our deepest feelings and sense of need – so that we feel understood as we articulate these words. They can also increase our sensitivity to the struggles of others: if you don't feel you want to pray this way today, you can think of someone else in need who does and pray this psalm on their behalf.

There is a shocking honesty and directness here, which we may find disconcerting, yet also liberating. The complaint about God's apparent negligence and indifference is addressed directly to God – who is still 'Yhwh my God' (v. 3). So instead of despair and resignation, the speaker appeals urgently to Yhwh to take action.

Some scholars try to fill in the gap between verses 4 and 5: they suggest that the speaker experienced a change for the better in their circumstances – or else a word from God (perhaps through a priest, as they prayed this psalm in the temple), assuring them of God's continued commitment and future saving help. This is possible, but speculative. It may be simplest to see the closing verses as a deliberate act of trust that God will act, even though the present struggles and suffering are continuing. Experiences of agonised despair and joyful hope coexist in a bewildering tension; on this occasion, hope gets the final word.

6 Speaking well

The significance of this beautiful psalm is underlined by its position: it is placed at the centre, the focal point, of another particular group (Psalms 15—24). It delights in aspects of God's creation and also in Yhwh's teaching (*Torah*), reminding us of the priorities we noticed in the Psalter's opening statements (Psalm 1:1–3). The power and significance of expression, particularly through words, is a theme running through this psalm.

Verses 1–6 highlight the 'words' of creation, especially as we look up to the skies. The heavens overhead proclaim to all of us in silent speech; their mysterious, wordless voice calls for our attention, announcing God's glorious splendour. The sun is rising today, and it rises every day, bringing light and warmth, enabling us to live and to experience another day of grace.

A change in tempo signals a change in topic in verses 7–11, as the focus shifts abruptly to the 'words' of scripture. Now the object of delight is another source of light, warmth and growth: Yhwh's instruction (*Torah*). Yhwh has given testimony, commands and declarations which are true and reliable – they have a delicious taste to be savoured and should be prized above all else. The regular, stately rhythm of these verses suggests that embracing this *Torah* can bring order to life.

Finally, in the closing verses, attention turns to our own speech: 'the words of my mouth'. As we pray with the psalmist, we realise that our words often lack the beauty, purity and integrity celebrated in the previous verses. So the psalm turns from declaring truths to ending with prayer: a longing to produce good words that come from good thoughts. The way forward is to look to Yhwh, the strong protector who is also redeemer. The word used for 'redeemer', *ga'al*, portrays God as acting like a powerful next of kin committed to putting things right for a family member who is in trouble or wronged (like Boaz, the *go'el* in the book of Ruth).

For those of us involved in Christian ministry and leadership, much of our work involves words: leading worship, preaching, conversations, meetings, emails, writing something for a local newsletter. Let's pray that we can take those opportunities to speak words that heal, inspire, nourish and liberate, bringing light and hope.

Guidelines

- Psalm 1 offers the striking image of the fruitful tree. Does this or any images from the other psalms we've read particularly resonate with you? Try exploring one of these images prayerfully; let it touch your emotions as well as your thinking.

- Do you find that the Psalter's association with King David enriches your reading and understanding of these psalms in certain ways? Or does it seem more of a distraction?

- How do you respond to the Psalter's call to be one of the people who are 'the righteous'? If you had to explain what this means and looks like to someone else, what words would you choose?

- Those of us who don't live under threat of danger or violence can find the anger and hostility towards enemies expressed in some psalms hard to stomach. If you feel that way, a solution may be to connect more closely with people today (near at hand, or further afield) whose lives really are lived under similar threats. How might you do that in ways that help you learn from their experience and further your understanding of these angry psalms?

- Psalm 8 is the only biblical text which can be found on the moon – inscribed on a disc deposited there by the Apollo 11 astronauts. The various texts on the disc were chosen by world leaders, to express what humanity believes and values; why do you think the Pope chose this particular psalm?

- As you experience the vivid words of the psalms, see what situations in today's world (close to home, or further afield) they bring to mind. Pray for those places and people.

1 Anguish and assurance

Psalm 22

Whose voice do we hear in this psalm? For many Christians, this is the voice of Jesus, speaking the opening verse from the cross (Mark 15:34; Matthew 27:46). But Jesus was quoting and inhabiting someone else's words.

As with many other psalms, the language used is powerful, vivid and unspecific. The precise details behind all the images are unclear. This innocent sufferer, 'groaning' (v. 1) with pain and distress, perhaps also in angry protest, might be physically ill or psychologically tormented; overwhelmed by enemies or shattered by threatening events. God, enthroned and exalted, seems far distant from one who feels squashed in the dirt (vv. 3, 6). The imagery could fit King David and some of his successors, or other godly individuals down the years – or perhaps the people of Israel as a whole. Jesus and the gospel writers see it fitting Jesus particularly well.

As we saw in Psalm 13, we also find here a sudden turning point towards the end (in the middle of verse 21). Now the outlook changes, with far less focus on self and immediate personal crisis; instead, we find concern for the poor, the nations and the future. The generations yet to come (vv. 30–31) speak of life, in contrast to the images of death which have dominated the earlier verses. Feasting is promised, and praise is mentioned four times. Does the speaker sense (perhaps through a word from someone else) a new hope and assurance? Or is this simply a statement of trust that change for the better will come eventually, in spite of the current struggles?

The gospel writers highlight the physical agony of Jesus' death, along with the torment of mockery and also the casting of lots for his clothes – all details expressed in Psalm 22. They don't quote the more hopeful verses at the end of the Psalm (although Hebrews 2:12 does put one of them on the lips of Jesus); yet they hint at hope, with the centurion's words and the tearing of the temple curtain (Mark 15:38–39). Like many who first heard the gospels, we recognise their references to Psalm 22 and perhaps are set thinking: 'How does the rest of that psalm go – and how does it end?' Despite the agonies so vividly portrayed, it is new life, hope and celebration that have the final word.

2 Well-being: 'for you are with me'

We noticed a sudden change of tone towards the end of Psalm 22, with despair giving way to exuberant hope. A similar contrast can be found in the middle of Psalm 23, but here the change moves in the opposite direction: the serenity and assurance of a contented life among still waters and green pastures is suddenly displaced by disturbing images of a dark valley, death and the presence of enemies. Life continues to present challenges and threats. Yet this is not the last word – despite acknowledging these dangers, the speaker soon reverts to assurance and trust. Now the words are addressed directly to 'you', reaching out in faith more personally to God. Yhwh is named in the opening and closing verses; keeping close to Yhwh in all life's delights and upheavals is what matters.

As often in Hebrew poems, this one has a high point right at the centre: 'for you are with me' (v. 4). The sense of God being with God's people is a theme that runs throughout our Bible (Genesis 28:15, 20; Jeremiah 1:8; Matthew 1:23; 28:20; Revelation 21:3). God is present and active: sometimes leading (vv. 2–3), sometimes following (v. 6); guiding, defending, anointing; providing essential food and drink for needy sheep and also, as the imagery changes, hosting a feast for honoured guests (vv. 2, 5).

In the Old Testament, kings and other rulers are sometimes depicted as 'shepherds' who fail in their responsibilities (Jeremiah 23:1–6; Ezekiel 34:1–16). This psalm 'of David' acknowledges that everyone, however famous or powerful, needs to recognise and submit to a higher shepherd, a greater king.

This psalm gives some good indications of what 'well-being' means. Basic needs are met (food, water, safety from threats). More than that, in verse 5 we find the experience of generous hospitality, probably a meal shared with others (perhaps even with former enemies) where this guest receives affirmation and feels valued. There is the physical activity of walking, along with a general sense of direction, purpose and hope for the future. In all this, the *nephesh* (inner life, sometimes translated 'soul', v. 3) is restored through relationship with Yhwh and through worship in Yhwh's 'house'. Noticing and being thankful for all these blessings is what generates a sense of well-being.

3 Where God and humans meet

Psalm 24

Many of the psalms we have been reading speak in very personal terms; we might forget that some were used in corporate worship. Psalm 24 gives a glimpse of worshippers, maybe a procession up to the temple in Jerusalem, perhaps carrying the ark of the covenant to celebrate a festival or a victory in battle (1 Chronicles 15—16 might come to mind). Or else it could depict Yhwh returning to Jerusalem after abandoning the city during the exile. As often in the Psalms, the language used is not specific enough for us to be sure about the details.

In this psalm's final section (vv. 7–10), God is invited to enter the space that humans inhabit, seemingly a town or city. Those who guard it are called to open up and welcome the arriving king; they respond by asking the identity of this one who seeks entry. Those approaching then identify the king as Yhwh, the strong one, mighty in battle. The call to 'lift up your heads' may be suggesting a need for bigger gates, in order to accommodate such a big God!

In the middle section (vv. 3–6), humans are invited to enter the space that God inhabits, probably the tabernacle or temple on Mount Zion in Jerusalem. Seeking God's 'face', the favourable gaze of Yhwh on the worshipper, is encouraged – but is not to be done casually or taken lightly. Here (as in Psalm 15), serious self-examination is urged before taking the risk of approaching this holy God. A life-changing commitment to purity and truthfulness is part of what God requires.

Where does this meeting of God and humans take place? In the place that the sovereign Yhwh has created and still owns – not just the spiritual realms, but the physical earth, with all its physical people (vv. 1–2). God is not invading the world humans live in; it already belongs to God. The world we inhabit can often feel insecure and unstable; yet Yhwh is like a skilled engineer, able to build secure foundations even on a marshy site. All its people are invited to acknowledge this, join the procession and worship the maker and sustainer of this world. In so doing, they will learn to treasure and preserve the world from chaos, just as the God they worship does.

4 Experiencing grace

Here is one of the psalms of thanksgiving, where the promise to give thanks and praise, which we have heard in some of the lament psalms (e.g. Psalm 13:5–6; 22:22, 25–26), becomes truly fulfilled. In this kind of psalm, we learn that God has acted, saving from enemies (Psalm 18), illness (Psalm 30) or sin (Psalm 32); the response is an outpouring of gratitude. The title of Psalm 34 points to an incident in the life of David, when King Saul was trying to kill him, and he attempted to hide in Philistine territory (1 Samuel 21:10—22:1). It was a crisis moment and a narrow escape; the psalm urges us to express gratitude after those kinds of experiences.

This is one of the psalter's eight 'acrostic' psalms: verse 1 begins with the Hebrew letter 'A', verse 2 with the Hebrew 'B' and so on through the alphabet. We don't know why the writers occasionally chose this form; perhaps it was to help people teach and memorise the words; perhaps it was like an 'A-to-Z', giving a full, rounded picture. Or perhaps it was just a bit of creative fun.

The first half of this psalm is full of testimony, about being saved from disaster by Yhwh. It invites the reader to share in the resultant rejoicing. Then, from verse 11, it changes into a wisdom psalm, seeking to live well in response to God's saving grace; we are invited to join in learning how best we can do that.

Imperatives abound, one after another: 'look to him... taste and see... depart from evil and do good'. They encourage and challenge us to take action. Various verbs in the Hebrew intensive form are also found here, urging us strongly to 'extol, boast, glorify, exalt, seek peace'. Here is passionate wholeheartedness.

Many of the psalms we have been reading speak in the voice of an individual, 'I'. Sometimes this individual voice might be a worship leader speaking on behalf of all the people together; we cannot be sure. But Psalm 34 reminds us clearly of the corporate nature of belonging to Yhwh: other people are addressed, using plural verbs; they are called to join in with what the speaker is expressing (vv. 2–3, 7–11, 15–19, 22). We praise God together, suffer affliction and broken hearts together, learn together, experience God's saving grace together, trust Yhwh together.

5 Experiencing agony

The contrast between yesterday's reading (Psalm 34) and this one is striking. Here we find no sense of a burden lifted, no relief at divine rescue. Instead, God seems to be distant, even angry – one of the encircling enemies, firing painful arrows into the speaker's body (v. 2), adding to the torment and crushing sense of isolation. Illness, sinfulness, enemies – all press in, threatening to overwhelm. The heart (v. 8) is a person's core, where not only feeling but also thinking and deciding take place; 'tumult' there suggests both mental and emotional anguish.

Awareness of sin is a feature of this psalm (vv. 3–5, 18). We've heard previous psalms reject 'the wicked' and we've noted the dangers of self-righteousness that can result from such an attitude. But here we find a keen sense of the speaker's own weakness, including failings and mistakes which are openly acknowledged to God. Honest self-awareness is one of the signs of maturity and humility.

Are sin and suffering connected? That's a complex issue. The idea that suffering must always be caused by sin is an oppressive one, which the book of Job powerfully rejects. But in psalms such as this one, the speaker has a strong conviction that their own sin has produced this current suffering (vv. 5–8, 17–18; compare 32:3–5). Physical, mental and emotional agony are all seen as arising from that sin, which needs to be repented of. The speaker is looking to God with openness and honesty (vv. 15, 18), suggesting a way forward (vv. 21–22). But the pain is not resolved at this point. For a celebration of relief and healing, experienced through receiving God's forgiveness, we need to look elsewhere (see Psalm 32).

For anyone prone to self-blame, inhabiting this psalm could be damaging – they might wrongly blame themselves for physical illness or depression. But for other people, this psalm can be a valuable challenge – a holistic reminder that our own mistakes and sins may oppress and damage us, through the mental/emotional burden of guilt and through other physical outworkings. At times, this psalm may give us words to express our own feelings; at other times, it may remind us to pray with imagination for someone else currently battling with this kind of trauma.

6 Finale

Our roller-coaster ride through the experiences and emotions of book one of the Psalter finishes here, with its closing psalm. This one begins with *ashrē*, meaning 'happy' or 'fortunate' – the same word that opened Psalm 1. These matching bookends indicate that Psalms 1—41 are organised as a collection, perhaps also that this whole collection has shown what an *ashrē* life looks like.

Familiar themes from all the previous psalms emerge here. We get a further picture of the way of the righteous and the way of the wicked (highlighted in Psalm 1), and how the truly wise person keeps living with integrity, whatever the temptations and provocations. Once again, we glimpse sickness and a sense of sin and forgiveness; danger from enemies, even from one who seemed to be a friend; the need to cry out for Yhwh's mercy and to trust in Yhwh's favour. There is also a promise that the blessing and contentment of *ashrē* is experienced through being considerate to those who are poor or helpless (v. 1). Like most of those in book one, this psalm is headed 'David's'.

What type of psalm is this? Is it a complaint arising from a current crisis? Or a thanksgiving, looking back after a crisis has been resolved? The difficulty we have in answering such questions decisively indicates that we should be wary of trying to categorise psalms too precisely into different types. Sometimes more than one form of writing is found within a single psalm.

Each of the Psalter's five books closes with a brief doxology, a burst of praise which directs our gaze away from self and the immediate situation and redirects it towards God. Yhwh is the 'God of Israel', committed to his people in covenant relationship. So those who pray these words can proclaim a sense of confidence and of being upheld in God's presence. In response to divine grace, they are called to 'bless' God (v. 13). Blessing is about freely and generously giving your best, proclaiming good things to another whom you love and are committed to; for us to bless God means giving God our thanks and praise. So despite its many laments, book one closes with praise – as befits the Hebrew title for the Psalter as a whole (*Tehillim*, meaning 'Praises'). The closing words invite us to respond with an emphatic double *amen* – 'yes, yes!'

Guidelines

- Did any of these psalms particularly catch your attention? Explore the reasons why. Is there a particular phrase or idea which stands out?

- What is God like, according to these psalms? Which aspects of God's character do they highlight? How does that shape your understanding of God? (We noticed that Psalm 34 is an acrostic. Try writing an A–Z of God's qualities and actions, as a creative bit of serious fun!)

- How might Psalms 8 and 24 help us navigate today's climate crisis? What kinds of attitudes and actions can they foster in us, which may be relevant in our response to this global emergency? If time allows, you might also reflect on Psalm 33 and Psalm 104 (which we'll consider more when we reach book four).

- Jesus seems to have memorised some or all of Psalm 22 – meaning he could call it to mind whenever he needed it. You might like to memorise one verse from a psalm each day, or even one whole psalm. Try revisiting it at times during the day, so you can inhabit and pray it afresh in different situations.

- From the earliest times, the Psalms have been treasured by Christians and central in Christian worship. How much do they feature in the patterns of worship in your church? Do you feel the balance is about right, or does it need adjusting?

- In any church congregation or small group, there is likely to be someone whose present experience is one of rejoicing and another who is in a season of lament. Can we minister to both these people, in a single service or sermon? How can the Psalms help in this?

FURTHER READING

Diane Bergant, *Psalms 1—72* (Liturgical Press, 2013).

Jerome Creach, *Discovering the Psalms: Content, interpretation, reception* (SPCK, 2020).

Nancy deClaisseé-Walford, Rolf A. Jacobson and Beth LaNeel Tanner, *The Book of Psalms* (Eerdmans, 2014).

John Goldingay, *Psalms: Volume one (1—41)* (Baker Academic, 2006). Volume two and three covering Psalm 42—89 and 90—150 are also available.

Jonathan Magonet, *A Rabbi Reads the Psalms* (SCM, 2004).

Reading the Bible interculturally

George M. Wieland

There is no view from nowhere. Everyone who reads or hears the Bible does so from a specific social and cultural location. It can be startling to discover what is seen in the same text by people who are looking at it from different vantage points.

New Zealand (Aotearoa in the indigenous Māori language) is home to an increasingly diverse population. The largest city, Auckland, is hyper-diverse, with large Māori and Pacific Island populations and a diminishing proportion of people of European ancestry, set to be outnumbered within a few years by Auckland's growing Asian population.

What a superb context in which followers of Jesus of all cultures could grow together in their knowledge of God and flourish in life and witness. Sadly, however, relationships between majority culture churches and other groups are often awkward. It is not just a matter of language. There is mutual incomprehension when what seems self-evident within one culture appears strange or even offensive to another. We desperately need to understand each other better. Could the Bible itself be a shared space in which that could happen?

An Intercultural Bible Reading project was developed at an Auckland theological college. Reading groups drawn from various cultures read selected Bible passages and simply talked about them together. Over the next two weeks we shall listen in on those conversations with groups of Māori, Samoan, Ni-Vanuatu, Fijian, Indian and Sri Lankan, Burmese, Chinese, Filipino and other readers. There is a lot to be learned about the Bible, its readers and its effects in different contexts.

Some passages need more than one day to explore. Take the opportunity to conduct your own intercultural reading experiment by reading the passage each day in a different translation or language. Do you pick up different nuances?

Unless otherwise stated, Bible quotations are taken from the NIV.

1 Jesus knew his name

Luke 19:1–10

Several groups read the same text, the story of Jesus and Zacchaeus, but they did not all hear the same things. There was a group of young male university students, heading (they hoped) into reasonably well-paid careers. What really got them going was the topic of money. How much of his wealth did Zacchaeus give away? Did he have to? Do we have to? We keep hearing about 'good news to the poor' but what if we're not poor – is the gospel for us as well? Clearly the Bible was stirring discomfort in those materially privileged young people and causing them to wrestle with questions about how their anticipated salaries and careers related to discipleship and salvation.

There were two groups of older women, in different parts of the country. Interestingly, both highlighted the theme of acceptance: Jesus accepted someone whom others hadn't and whom the crowd didn't make room for. The comment was made that you only really get to know someone when you go to their home and see them as they are. Are there hints of a decline in the practice of 'pastoral visitation', often denigrated as 'drinking cups of tea with old ladies', in favour of a system of pastoral care by appointment? To people who feel unvalued and sidelined in a world and even in churches that seem to be passing them by, the Bible was offering reassurance of Jesus' acceptance.

And there was a striking result from a group of young people from Ethiopian refugee families. As each in turn mentioned what they had noticed in the story, there was one point that almost everyone in that group cited as important: 'Jesus knew his name.' As a close second, most of them found it significant that Jesus had actually gone into Zacchaeus' house. For those young migrants, struggling for identity and belonging in a country that treats them as aliens and where no one knows (and few would bother to pronounce!) their names, the reading of that passage ignited surprise and delight. Jesus not only knew the name of the strange man who didn't fit in with the crowd, but by stepping through Zacchaeus' door, he broke down the divide that separated the little world of that home from the large world of the community around it. A community that, until then, Zacchaeus had not been able to belong to.

2 Obedience is the proof of love

Genesis 22:1–19

One reading group was located not in New Zealand but in a Southeast Asian country whose population is predominantly Buddhist. Some years earlier, a local man became a believer in Jesus and started a church in his village. After he died, the church was left without a leader and many of the members drifted away. A small group, however, including two of the pastor's daughters, continued to meet in a home and encourage each other to stay faithful.

When they read the story of Abraham's willingness to sacrifice his son, Isaac, it was his total and unquestioning obedience that impressed them. It proved that Abraham loved God so much that when God gave him the most precious gift, his son Isaac, he was willing to give him back to God. Everything, including family, is given by God, so when God asks for it back, it must be returned.

In that Buddhist environment, many families earn merit by gifting a son to the temple to train as a monk. One of the women in the group spoke in similar terms of offering her son for God's service from the moment of his birth. He had indeed followed that path and when he grew up he travelled throughout the country as an evangelist and Christian teacher.

Another participant suggested that since God had already proved that he could give Abraham a son, he could trust that if he gave that son back, God would be able to give him several more. In fact, God did make Abraham the father of many nations. The lesson taken from that was that such costly obedience is what we have to do to gain blessings from God.

What all this meant for Isaac did not enter the conversation until the New Zealander present posed the question. The group replied that he would have obeyed his father and submitted to being offered. As a good father, Abraham would have taught his son obedience, but also to trust that God would find a way to help him no matter how impossible it seemed. For the founding pastor's daughters, this reinforced the importance of following their father's teaching.

Elements of this story can seem disturbing from a modern western perspective. Evidently, though, they had meaning for this group, within both the general Buddhist environment and their particular context as a small group of believers holding on to their faith in challenging circumstances.

3 What sort of sacrifice?

Genesis 22:1–19

This passage (the same as yesterday's) was read by a group of Nepali immigrants in Auckland. Some had very recently come to believe in Jesus, others had already been believers before leaving Nepal, but all had been brought up in a Hindu environment and had Hindu families.

The story of Abraham prompted conversation about faith. One participant spoke of the earnestness with which they prayed and tried to exercise faith when they wanted something from God, such as a child, a job or a visa. They felt an affinity with Abraham, who, they assumed, must have prayed for years for the gift of a son. But as the discussion moved back and forth between the biblical passage and their own experience, they identified two points at which faith is challenged. One was when what they prayed for was received. Does faith diminish when there is no longer the urgency of dependence on God? The other was if that for which they have exercised faith is taken away. Could Abraham – and would they – continue to trust God in the face of such disappointment and confusion?

The fact that Abraham's faith was tested in the context of family relationships resonated strongly with the group. In Nepali culture, all significant events involve family gatherings with religiously prescribed rituals, such as receiving *tika*, the red mark on the forehead that signifies religious devotion. For first-born sons, there are particular responsibilities that carry significance for the well-being of the family in this life and beyond. There were tears as the group spoke of the pain for them and their families when they felt they could no longer participate in those ceremonies. It involved sacrifice, perhaps not of a child but certainly of relationships and standing in the family. And yet, experiences were shared of God providing solutions in surprising ways so that important events could take place and relationships could be maintained without involving the young believers in what they understood to be the worship of gods they no longer served.

Who decides what is Christian behaviour in such situations? Instructions formulated in cultural contexts where religion is a private, individual matter are not adequate to guide life and witness in communal and holistic environments. As those Nepali believers themselves engaged together with the Bible's story of Abraham's obedience and God's provision, relating it to their own experiences, ways of faithfulness and trust in their context began to be discerned.

4 Not a Sunday-school God!

The young Māori followers of Jesus who read this passage (again, the same as yesterday's) were exploring together what it would mean for them to be both authentically Māori and faithfully Christian. This is a challenging journey in a context where the faith they profess is inextricably linked in their history to colonisation and its continuing destructive effects on indigenous people, language and culture. They were questioning and wrestling as they attempted to disentangle their knowledge of God from colonial structures and attitudes and listen afresh to the wisdom of their people transmitted through many generations.

A willingness to interrogate the text was evident in the first response to the reading: 'Surely not! That's out of character for God.' It was deeply troubling both that God should require the sacrifice of a child and even that God would want to 'test' someone. There was animated discussion about the tension between their prior ideas of who God was or should be like and the God that they were encountering in the Bible passage. Having begun by challenging the text, however, the conversation shifted to receiving the challenge that the text, in turn, presented to them. What if it was not the biblical story but their assumptions about what God would and would not do that were in need of correction? Were they willing to lay down their received ideas about God in order to know God more authentically? A posture emerged of humble respect and awe, and an openness to being confronted by a God beyond their comprehension.

What, then, might be the purpose of the test that God set for Abraham? One participant drew on a Māori concept of spiritual alignment to God, pictured as a stream that flows to us from the source of life. That alignment might be disrupted by other things and at such times we are challenged to realign ourselves to God, putting the relationship with God in first place over all other relationships. That may indeed require sacrifice.

The group reflected again on their initial instinctive unwillingness to conceive of God making such extreme demands. Where had that come from? Had they been conditioned to think of God in superficially pleasant and undemanding terms, a 'sunshine and rainbows' Sunday-school God? If they wanted to grow in their knowledge of God, they would have to be willing to sit in a place of discomfort.

5 Perseverance

The Southeast Asian villagers found immense encouragement in the example of the four friends who brought the paralysed man to Jesus. They persevered! Many of their small community of believers had apparently given up on their faith, or at least on their participation in the church. After losing their founding pastor, it had been hard to keep going as they faced challenges of health, finances and family problems. Well, the friends in this passage also encountered many obstacles but they didn't turn back. Jesus is the solution to our problems. If we turn around when it becomes difficult, we won't reach him. If we keep going with determination and patience, we will meet him and receive the help we need.

The four friends in this passage also demonstrate the value of working as a team. One member of the Southeast Asian village confessed that were it not for the small group that met to worship and encourage each other, they would not have survived. It takes all of them working together to get one person to stand up!

They observed that it was the humble and weak who received forgiveness and healing from God. There were highly educated people there, the scribes, but for all their knowledge they failed to recognise God when he was standing there in front of them. Testimonies were shared of healings that had confounded the doctors. One woman, after three months in hospital being treated unsuccessfully for a number of chronic conditions, was sent home because the doctor could do no more for her. A month later, he called her in for a blood test that showed a remarkable improvement. He asked her what medicine she had been taking. 'None,' she said. 'I just prayed to God and asked Jesus to heal me.' The astonished doctor had no further treatment to offer. He told her to go home and keep being a child of God. That's what she was still doing 30 years later.

The Māori group noted the order in which Jesus had performed the healing – first forgiveness, then physical restoration. If something is wrong in the spirit, that has to be put right before external healing can take place. This spoke to current attempts in the nation and the churches to address past and present injustices in the relationship between Māori and the European colonisers. Spiritual obstructions in the form of unresolved sin and heart attitudes must be dealt with before a just society can be achieved.

6 Who won't you eat with?

The Tamil group read the opening verses of this passage and immediately recognised social and cultural prejudice. No one interpreted the criticism directed against Jesus for eating with 'sinners' as an example of moral scruples about associating with ungodly people. What they saw was the kind of social separation that they were so familiar with between castes in their Indian and Sri Lankan communities. One group looked down with distaste on another and, in particular, would not eat with them. Sadly, they agreed that such attitudes were prevalent not only in society but also in their churches.

Christians of other cultures were surprised, even dismayed, to hear of the continuing effects of caste in how people relate to one another within the church. We found ourselves implicated, however, when the conversation moved on to the racial prejudice that the Tamil believers had all experienced in New Zealand. The same critique applies: Christians who exhibit such attitudes and ways of relating to others show that their behaviour is shaped not by the Bible's teaching but by quite different considerations.

The parable of the lost sheep had a particular resonance for one reader. He was impacted by the picture of Jesus as the shepherd going after a sheep that had somehow been scattered and finding it in the place where it had gone. That, he said, had been his experience. He was part of the Tamil diaspora, scattered to various parts of the world. But God had come after him and found him in New Zealand! That is the testimony of large numbers of Indian, Sri Lankan and other diaspora communities in places to which they have migrated. What would it do to our practice of local mission if we could see not only the 'lost sheep' who find themselves in our neighbourhood, but also the good shepherd who is here seeking them?

As for the story of the lost coin, the Tamil group felt the pain sharply. 'That lady must have lost a piece of silver from her *thaali* [the necklace that the bridegroom ties round the neck of his bride]. That's a terrible omen. She has to do everything to search for it.' That perspective helped the rest of us to grasp more profoundly the significance of that which was lost, the eagerness of the seeker and the joy when it was found.

Guidelines

- How well do you know your context? In our rapidly changing world, local populations can change around us without us noticing. Explore the contexts in which you live, work or worship. Demographic information such as census statistics is readily accessible, but you can supplement those by simply walking around, looking and listening. Take a walk, if you are able to, and pray as you go for an open heart towards those whose lives are intersecting with your own.

- The student who read the Bible with the Ethiopian young people (day one) had been a member of her church for seven years before she discovered that an Ethiopian congregation worshipped in the same building on Saturdays. It is not unusual for immigrant Christian groups to meet in existing church buildings, often at different times to the church's regular worship. Does your church have such an arrangement with any immigrant group? Do you know them? What steps could be taken to move up the relationship scale from tenants to partners to members together?

- 'Jesus knew his name.' It takes effort to learn to pronounce a name in a different language, but what does that effort indicate? Whose name could you learn?

- We have read the Bible this week with some groups for whom eating together is highly significant. Who might you eat with this week? Is there anyone you are reluctant to eat with? Why?

- Without exception, all the students who participated in the Intercultural Bible Reading project found that their relationships with the groups they read with deepened significantly through the process. One student, a leader in a large city church, set about using the approach to foster interaction and enhance understanding between the many different cultural groups in her church. Could this method be fruitful in your context? What would it take to begin?

1 What did you miss?

Luke 15:11–32

New Testament professor Mark Allen Powell reports a fascinating Bible reading experiment in his book *What Do They Hear? Bridging the gap between pulpit and pew* (Abingdon, 2007). Teaching in North America, he liked to set his class a simple exercise in recall. They had to read a familiar Bible story, then shut their Bibles and, in pairs, one student retold the story and the other listened for accuracy. On one occasion the passage he set was Luke 15:11–32, the parable of the prodigal son. As might be expected with such a well-known story, the level of accuracy was quite high, except for one thing. Almost all the students omitted one element that is there in the text: the famine. Have you ever noticed it? It's there in verse 14, but they had missed it.

Later, Powell had the opportunity to teach in the Russian city of St Petersburg. He set the same exercise, with strikingly different results. Of those students, 86% mentioned the famine. That was not difficult to explain. During World War II, their city had suffered a brutal siege which cut off its food supply. Over one million people died of starvation. Famine was a harsh reality in their recent history. No wonder they noticed it when it appeared in the Bible. For the American students, however, famine was so far outside their experience that even when they read it in the text, it did not register.

The text also states that the younger brother 'squandered' his inheritance (v. 13). That was faithfully reported by 100% of the American students, but, strangely, only 34% of the Russian group. How, then, was the young man's desperate situation to be explained? The American students were unanimous: he had been irresponsible; it was his own fault. For the Russians, however, what he had done with his money was of far less relevance than the fact that a famine had afflicted that region. He was suffering because of circumstances beyond his control, and his sin had been to try to be self-sufficient instead of living interdependently within the family where security was to be found.

That illustrates powerfully the significance of both location (geographical, historical, social) and cultural attitudes (individualist or communal) in what readers see – and fail to see – in the Bible and how it speaks to them. Over the next two days we shall discover how this passage engaged other groups of readers.

2 'I am the elder brother'

Of all the Bible passages discussed by groups participating in the Intercultural Bible Reading project, this was the one that consistently engaged people at a deep emotional level. It is a story of family dynamics that people intuitively mapped on to the realities of family life in their cultural contexts.

Two Fijian participants were so shocked by the younger son's demand for his father's will to be executed before he had even died that the leader had some difficulty in persuading them to remain in the group. They stayed and, in time, offered insight into why the father ran to meet his son when he returned. He had to get to him before the local people saw him because they would have driven him away for bringing such shame on the community.

Indian, Sri Lankan and Pakistani group members pictured extended family discussions before it was decided that the younger brother could take some of the family money and go elsewhere, reflecting the deliberations that preceded their own departure overseas. Perhaps it might be good for the family business!

There was sympathy for the elder brother. He couldn't go away because he had so much responsibility at home. He had worked diligently all his life, apparently without appreciation. In several groups, at least one person confessed, 'I am the elder brother.' There were stories from Chinese women of disparity in treatment between brothers, who were given whatever gifts, freedoms and opportunities they asked their parents for, and sisters, who were denied these things, no matter how hard they tried to please their parents. There was hurt and resentment against siblings, parents and God.

However, as the conversations continued, perspectives shifted. Why was the elder brother so bitter? It can't have been about the money – the younger son had already received his share, so now the elder son would inherit everything that remained (v. 31). It was about the relationship. His mentality was that of an employee of a demanding owner, not the child of a loving father. He complained that he had never been given anything, but had he even asked? Had he failed to recognise his father's kind and generous character? Lacking a relationship of love with his father, he was unable to share his father's joy or receive his brother with forgiveness, and he stayed outside. He, too, had left the family.

3 How weird is that?

Luke 15:11–32

Most of the reading groups considered themselves to be Christian. This was not the case for one group of staff and patrons of a popular urban cafe. When their Christian friend asked if they would be willing to read and talk about parts of the Bible to help him with some research, they were intrigued and agreed to participate. Most were young, educated, majority-culture professionals with no religious commitment. They decided to describe their group as 'atheists and non-God-botherers'.

They found many things in the story odd, but one element that evoked no surprise was the younger son asking for his inheritance in advance and heading out into the world. In an economic environment where it is very difficult to get going in business or home ownership unless you can draw on 'the bank of mum and dad', it makes good sense to get access to money when it is needed instead of waiting until the parents' death. The suggestion that the father might have been upset when his younger son left home was queried. He might have been proud of his son for having the courage to strike out on his own.

Another key moment, when the son was welcomed back, provoked an unexpected objection. 'They're happy, so they go out and kill an animal! How weird is that? I don't do that when I'm happy.' The statement that the son had been dead and was now alive again was also puzzling – you don't consider somebody dead just because they leave home!

Many of the Christian students engaged in this Bible Reading project shared culture, education and language with those urban professionals, but when they approached the biblical passage they found themselves in completely different symbolic and interpretive worlds. With the groups from Asian or Pacific contexts, however, there was recognition that for all their differences they inhabited the same biblical world.

And yet one of those 'atheists and non-God-botherers' offered this summary: 'That story, I believe, is about a person who was once in a good place and then became an undesirable, then he's being welcomed back. Which is possibly why Jesus was hanging out with those undesirable types, to get them back to the family, so to speak.' Precisely. For all the perplexity and cultural misunderstanding, the Bible, by the Spirit, had done its work and revealed Jesus.

4 What would keep you from eating?

'Would you have eaten?' In Samoan culture, almost every event centres on food. It is not surprising, then, that the statement that Saul did not eat or drink for three days got the attention of the Samoan reading group. They agreed that even if they were struck blind, they would still eat! The shock that Saul experienced must have been more profound than losing his sight. Was it the realisation that he had done wrong? There were those in the group who had drifted from their traditional Samoan church upbringing and done things they were now ashamed of. It was hard to go back and face the people whom they had hurt. Was that part of what Saul was going through?

The urban cafe group was also puzzled by Saul's fast, but for other reasons. They couldn't understand why not being able to see meant that he couldn't eat. Did the people he was travelling with not give him any food? They concluded, as had the Samoan group, that something deep and internal was going on in Saul. Perhaps it was a kind of detox, a cleansing of the hatred and the bad he was doing through a period of self-assessment.

The Burmese group appreciated the connection between Saul's physical and spiritual conditions. His intense hatred, 'breathing out murderous threats' against the followers of Jesus (v. 1), revealed a spiritual blindness that was more dangerous than physical blindness because it kept him from a relationship with God. Accordingly, God first fed Saul's spiritual body with forgiveness and fellowship and only then fed his physical body.

The conversation in the urban cafe moved to Saul's response. If it had been Jesus who inflicted this horrible experience on him, why would Saul then want to follow him? Perhaps, they thought, Saul needed a wake-up call to make him realise that he had stop and do things differently, just as all of us need to be stopped in our tracks if our lives are heading in the wrong direction.

'I wish God would talk to me like that. I've been trying to speak to him for years and waiting for him to talk back.' That surprising admission came at the end of the urban cafe conversation. Who could have guessed that beneath the urbane secular exterior there was such a longing to hear God? Perhaps as they pondered Saul's story, it was beginning to be fulfilled.

5 Everyone needs an Ananias

Acts 9:10–19

'In a way he almost talks back to God!' In many church youth groups, Ananias' push back against God's instruction to go and find Saul would seem natural. However, for the Chinese young people reading this passage, it was startling. They were expected to obey their parents and teachers without questioning; so how could someone – a disciple – argue with God? Ananias seemed to have a relationship with God that was different to theirs. He was so comfortable with God that he could talk openly with him, say to God exactly what he thought and come through that conversation to a place of courageous obedience.

They noticed a lot of surprise and confusion in the passage, for both Saul and Ananias. That resonated with some. They also felt confused about what God seemed to be doing or wanting them to do. It was comforting to see that even when the people involved did not understand what was going on, God was at work in amazing ways. There is a big picture even if they don't see it at the time.

Across the groups, the question of why God had to bring Ananias into the story was raised. Why did God not simply speak to Saul directly, as he had before? A group of women from Vanuatu in the south Pacific spoke about one of the first missionaries to one of their islands. He had been killed, but years later there was a reconciliation between the people of that place and the missionary's family, establishing a relationship that continues to this day. Perhaps, they suggested, Saul had to experience being healed by the very disciples he was persecuting. The Chinese young people suggested that Ananias also needed that experience to teach him how to love and forgive his enemies, and to see how God is able to turn someone's life around. In the urban cafe, the idea of mutual learning was attractive. Two very different people are brought together so that each can learn and be altered.

There was gratitude for those who had been the 'Ananias' in some people's lives. A participant in the Filipino group shared her experience. She had been far from God and antagonistic towards the church when she came across someone whose beautiful character and warmth softened her attitude. When this new friend invited her to attend church with her, she went and her life began to change.

6 Who are you in the story?

Acts 9:1–19

Could there be any sympathy for Saul the persecutor? In two groups, examples of hostility to Christians were described where those who experienced the persecution may have shared some responsibility for it. A Burmese woman confessed that she had hated Christians for years after being mistreated by a Christian family for whom she had worked. The Vanuatu group spoke about the killing of a Christian missionary. A local man had gone to work overseas for a white employer who had abused and humiliated him. When he got back to his island he swore that he would not permit any white person to set foot there, to protect his community from that brutality. Consequently, when a white man did arrive, he killed him, but not specifically because he was a Christian. Neither group wanted to explain Saul's actions in that way, but they cautioned against assuming that all hostility that Christians experience is because of their faith.

Many empathised with Ananias' struggle to change his attitude towards the persecutor. A young man shared the experience of his sister and brother-in-law. False accusations were made against them by someone who was trying to get them imprisoned. At first, the family asked God to cause some harm to the accuser to stop the attack, but they realised that was wrong. Instead, they began to pray for their persecutor's salvation and blessing.

When the Chinese young people were asked who they most identified with in the passage, one or two said Saul or Ananias, but most were quiet. Pressed for an answer, a young woman replied, 'No one, because I don't see myself as having a prominent role.' Nods around the room indicated wide agreement. In a communal culture that values humility and harmony, it is not necessarily a good thing to assume a leading role. So was there any place for them in the story? Certainly. 'I'm nobody special, but I identify with the nameless group – the courage they must have had to have Saul stay with them for a few days.' Have you ever noticed those heroes right at the end of the passage or given thought to what it took for them to welcome the one who had come to their city to destroy them (v. 19b)? Perhaps it is especially from the margins that it is possible to see and learn from those on the edges of the story.

Guidelines

The theological students who facilitated the groups observed that while they tended to assume some distance between themselves as readers and the text, supplying historical background, linguistic, literary and other information to enable them to interpret it, the readers in the group plunged right in. They found themselves in the text and read it with an immediacy of appropriation for their own lives.

- If you are among those who tend to read from a distance, try plunging right in! Pick one of the passages we have read, or another, and enter it with empathetic identification and openness to emotional response, questions and puzzlement. What does it do to you?

- The secular young professionals in their urban cafe are perhaps two or more generations away from habits of churchgoing or attendance at Sunday school and they come to the Bible perhaps for the first time with no knowledge of these stories and without the interpretive codes and symbols that are assumed in many churches. Who do you know like that? What cannot be assumed in your conversations with them?

- Yet, as we saw, such avowedly non-religious people may actually have a deep spiritual yearning and a desire for direction in their lives. Could the invitation to read the Bible together for mutual learning be a way to open conversations with them?

- Everyone needs an Ananias who is attentive to God, is available for God's prompting and has the courage to step out and make the connection with people in whom God is at work. For whom might you be an Ananias? If you have been given the privilege of such a role, what did you learn through it about God's grace and power, about other people and how God deals with them and about yourself?

FURTHER READING

Mark Allan Powell, *What Do They Hear? Bridging the gap between pulpit and pew* (Abingdon, 2007).

Jason Thomaskutty (ed.), *An Asian Introduction to the New Testament* (Fortress, 2022).

George M. Wieland, 'Cultivating Attentiveness: Formation for ministry through the practice of intercultural Bible reading', *Colloquium* 53.1 (2021), pp. 98–120.

Matthew 19—23

Andy Angel

In the previous issue, we looked at Matthew 15—18. Jesus now moves to the region of Judea (Matthew 19:1) and to Jerusalem (Matthew 21:10). Although the crowds are following him, opposition to his ministry intensifies. Those who would traditionally greet a dignitary with great pomp and circumstance treat Jesus with suspicion and anger. They are not quite sure how to handle him as they can see that the crowds (currently) love him and enjoy his continuing healing ministry and teaching. Jesus finds himself embroiled in controversies. Much of this is of his own making as he is unafraid to challenge leaders with their rejection of his ministry or to prophesy that they will come under God's judgement for their rejection of him. We end this series of studies on the rather dark-sounding notes of Jesus' criticisms of the Pharisees in Matthew 23 – a chapter which has many challenges for the contemporary interpreter.

However, in all of this, we meet the living Jesus – a Jesus who is unafraid to challenge people in order to bring them to repentance, receiving God's forgiveness and beginning to live new and transformed lives. Sometimes his words are quite shocking. The way in which he paints members of his audience into his parables, and into the roles of bad characters, hardly conforms to contemporary ideas of appropriate behaviour. His use of strong and blunt vocabulary would offend if we read it on the lips of most other people. However, in all the challenges and controversies that we will encounter, we need to realise that Jesus' purpose is to bring us to repentance, forgiveness and new life. As we read these stories, we need to identify creatively with the characters we find in them. Although we can have a tendency to identify with Jesus (and understandably so), sometimes it can be good to read the stories as the chief priests, the scribes or the Pharisees, and ask how Jesus' challenge to them speaks his challenge to us. Read this way, the stories of the gospels can come to sparkling (though very often uncomfortable) life. It is precisely in the discomfort where we find the light of Jesus breaking through and offering us a way into more of the life he longs for us all to lead.

Unless otherwise stated, Bible quotations are taken from the NRSV.

1 Pain and hope

Matthew 19:1–12

This must be one of the more difficult of Jesus' conversations to read for many people. Divorce is a painful subject because it is painful. Any breakdown of relationship is painful. Matthew may point out that the Pharisees were testing Jesus here, but they were realists as regards to divorce. The Torah accepted that it happened and regulated for divorce (Deuteronomy 24:1–4). Facing the difficult questions that arise around divorce settlements, the Pharisees tried to regulate the many tricky areas on which the Torah was silent. You can read some of this in the Mishnah Gittin. Famously, they debated acceptable grounds for divorce because the Torah said nothing on this.

Here, they ask Jesus his view on acceptable grounds for divorce. Jesus answers their question six verses later. *Porneia* (sexual immorality) is grounds for divorce. There is a lively debate among scholars as to what this specifically means and answers range from marriages which are banned in the Torah (see Leviticus 18) through to adultery. But Jesus does not focus on this.

Rather than focus on marital breakdown, Jesus focuses on God's vision. Jesus' words here are as close as he gets to disagreeing with anything in the Torah. He says that the regulations in Deuteronomy 24:1–14 were given because of the hardness of people's hearts, and that divorce was not part of God's vision for humanity. Jesus does not duck the difficult issue with which the Pharisees struggle. He answers their question, but he asks them to lift their eyes to a higher vision, and for that vision he takes them back to the beginning of the Torah. Jesus quotes Genesis 1:27 and 2:24 to illustrate that God makes marriages. God makes two people one, and so no one has the right to undo what God has made. Both the texts Jesus quotes are full of hope. The first speaks of men and women being the high point of God's creation and receiving the command to participate in God's work of creation in having children. The second speaks of the man and woman finding companionship together. Jesus asks all of us not to focus on the mess we make of creation, but on the vision God has for us to flourish in creation.

2 Learning by doing

Matthew 19:13–15

One of the frustrations of any teacher is the danger of surface-level learning. You can have people who love you and genuinely enjoy learning from you – but then put virtually nothing of it into practice. It is much easier to learn things as ideas to think about rather than as ideas to live by. True worship and genuine discipleship make us dig around our cultural foundations and, where they are found to be unstable, allow God to remove and replace them. This is what is happening in these verses.

Jesus has already taught his disciples that 'unless you change and become like children, you will never enter the kingdom of heaven' (18:3) and 'whoever becomes humble like this child is the greatest in the kingdom of heaven. Whoever welcomes one such child in my name welcomes me' (18:4–5). Some people acted as if these words were true. They brought children to Jesus for prayers and blessing as if he actually cared about them. The disciples were quite sure this was out of order. Literally, they rebuked the people who were doing this. Hmm. 'Whoever receives one single child like this…' The disciples may have heard the words. They may even have liked his words or, possibly, repeated them to others, but they clearly did not understand his words at anything other than a surface level because they put the exact opposite into practice – and Jesus points this out. He tells them to let the children to come to him 'for it is to such as these that the kingdom of heaven belongs' (v. 14).

This must have hurt the disciples a bit. In rebuking parents bringing children to Jesus, the disciples assumed they had the status and authority to do this. They also assumed that the children did not have the status necessary to be worthy of Jesus' attention. When Jesus tells them to let the children come, all this changes. Jesus gives the children status, and the disciples take a knock to their perceived status and authority. But as the disciples obey and let children come, Jesus lays much more solid foundations in their lives of faith because they become doers of his words and not merely hearers.

3 Blind spots

We all have them – areas of our lives where we do not see as clearly as we ought. Sometimes we are oblivious to them and are truly unaware of aspects of our characters. Sometimes we have an inkling, but we prefer not to go there. Other times, we are aware of failings but do our best to ignore them.

The man who comes to Jesus in this story is just like us – he has a blind spot. In many ways he is an amazing guy. He has never committed murder or adultery, or given false testimony. He has never stolen. He has always respected his parents. He loves others as himself. He even wants to know where he might still be lacking (v. 20). Jesus tells him and he finds it hard to take. The young man leaves grieving because he has many possessions and clearly does not want to part with them.

This young man knows the commandments well – but not perfectly. When Jesus lists the commandments that he agrees he has kept, he has to ask 'What do I still lack?' The young man could not see his blind spot. He was genuinely good in many ways with regard to property, as he had never stolen. However, he enjoyed possessing a great deal of property and somehow this affected his spirituality such that he'd forgotten the command not to covet: 'You shall not covet your neighbour's house; you shall not covet your neighbour's wife, or male or female slave, or ox, or donkey, or anything that belongs to your neighbour' (Exodus 20:17; Deuteronomy 5:21). Jesus offered him radical healing, but he found the medicine too bitter to swallow at that moment.

Too often we avoid the challenge of Jesus' teaching here by stating that this was only Jesus' command to that particular young man. We can safely ignore it as not relevant to us. But we cannot. Jesus' instruction to that young man is based on God's commandments to all of us. We are all called to be generous, and we can all have blind spots. For example, the fact that many of us live in relative wealth and prosperity does not negate the call to use our wealth to heal and help others in their poverty.

4 A discomforting challenge and a joyful vision

Matthew 19:23–30

We are not the first to try to wriggle out of the challenge of Jesus' teaching on wealth and poverty. His comment on the rich young man's reaction is tough: 'It is easier for a camel to go through the eye of a needle than for someone who is rich to enter the kingdom of God.' The disciples have given up everything to follow Jesus, so their reaction to Jesus' words is almost to give up (v. 25): 'Then who can be saved?'

Down the centuries, interpreters have tried to wriggle out of this one. Anselm (AD1033–1109) claimed that the eye of a needle was a gate in Jerusalem so narrow that camels had to take their baggage off to get through, but there is no evidence for this. A ninth-century AD manuscript changes one letter in the Greek word for 'camel' to make it mean 'rope' – which, though still difficult, is much easier to get through the eye of a needle. But that is changing Jesus' words, even if the copyist was sleepy and did it accidentally! The truth is that Jesus said something remarkably difficult for us. We like the idea of having great wealth but we also like the idea of entering the kingdom of heaven.

But Jesus is not as bleak as we are. He boldly states that rich people entering the kingdom of heaven is not impossible as nothing is impossible with God (v. 26). Given all that he has said up to this point, he clearly envisages God helping rich people become astoundingly generous and giving their wealth away. Jesus also calls his disciples to a much more positive outlook. To the disciples' general disbelief at Jesus' comments, Peter adds the mild rebuke that they have already given up everything to follow him (v. 27). Jesus asserts that they will not lose their reward and that on the great day when God renews all things, there will be quite a reversal of riches and poverty. These words function as a joyful vision and a warning: to those who hoard wealth for themselves, a warning; but to those who allow the God of the impossible to change our hearts and minds such that we give away what we have, a joyful vision.

5 Outrageous generosity

The key to understanding this parable lies in its context. It ends with the punchline: 'So the last will be first, and the first will be last' (v. 16). It begins with the conjunction 'for', which joins it to what comes before and implies that this parable explains it. What comes before is the punchline 'but many who are first will be last, and the last will be first' (19:30), which ends Jesus' answer to Peter about the rewards God gives those who give up possessions to follow Jesus. So, this parable is about how God rewards those who give up possessions to follow Jesus.

Depending on your outlook, the parable has either a sting in its tail or is infused with the most outrageous generosity. The kingdom of heaven is compared to a landowner hiring workers and the parable focuses on pay-time. Given the context, pay-time must represent the renewal of all things when God rewards those who have given up homes, relatives and property to follow Jesus. The grumpy workers, and the one Jesus speaks with (vv. 12–13), might represent the disciples being astounded at Jesus, and Peter telling Jesus just how much they had given up to follow him (19:25–27). The landowner rewards all who work in the vineyard with the full daily wage, regardless of the time they started. In other words, however much we give up for God, at whatever point in our lives we give God our all, God rewards us with the full blessing of his kingdom.

The parable does not shirk the challenge for all of us who follow Jesus to give up our all. Each of the workers does the same work in the same vineyard. Nor does the parable give us any space to moan at Jesus, like Peter, that we have given up so much for so long that we want to make sure our reward takes this into account. God looks on our giving up our all (whatever the amount in time and money) with delight and rewards every one of us with the highest pay – regardless of how long we have served him. God is outrageously generous, and not only should we not gainsay his outrageous generosity, but we should also imitate it in sharing our wealth with those who need it.

6 Naked ambition laid bare

In verses 17–19, Jesus gives an example of what it means that the last shall be first in his prophecy of his arrest, torture, mockery and crucifixion. In the humiliation and agony of these events, he will become the last, but, in his being raised from the dead, he will become first. Sadly, these truths are lost on some of his disciples and their relatives, as Zebedee's wife and sons, James and John, illustrate perfectly.

They come to Jesus, and the mother asks for special positions for her sons in the renewal of all things when the disciples sit on twelve thrones judging the tribes of Israel (compare 19:28) – the two thrones closest to Jesus. Her sons are clearly standing there as she makes her request, as Jesus asks them whether they can drink from the cup from which he will drink. In their eagerness for power and privilege, they answer that they can. Jesus responds with what will have been a disappointing reply – you may well not get the thrones you are asking for, but you will suffer as I do. When they hear all this, the other disciples are furious. Clearly, they are keen not to lose out on the positions of privilege and honour in Jesus' kingdom.

Jesus' response puts them all in their place. The kind of power you are seeking betrays you all as little better than Gentile despots – the kind whose power you are hoping to replace with the kingdom of heaven. Jesus highlights the hypocrisy of their desires. He then puts them straight: 'It will not be so among you' (v. 26). Instead, those who wish to be great must serve and those who wish to be first must become slaves to their fellow disciples. Jesus seems to be teaching the lessons 'the first shall be last…' and 'unless you change and become like children you will never enter the kingdom…' again. The disciples are only just beginning to let Jesus' vision get beneath the surface of their learning. Soon, though, they are going to learn a lesson that will both terrify them and utterly transform their lives, because Jesus will give his life as a ransom for many and so serve before being exalted, served and worshipped.

Guidelines

'This brings you humility and poverty.' As an advertising campaign, this would hardly sell an aftershave or perfume – let alone high-fashion clothing or a particular brand of car. Humility and poverty are very powerful, not because people generally desire them (like we do wealth, power and beauty) but because they really quite powerfully repel people. Few people are genuinely happy with low status. Most people want high status, even if only within their group (however low status that might be within society as a whole). Even fewer people aim for poverty.

So Jesus' teaching in this week's passages is quite hard to take on board. We are called to give up everything for him. Even if we remain living in a nice area, in a nice town, in a relatively wealthy country, we are to see our wealth as God's and not ours – and that means being willing to sell up and give it away if that is what God calls us to do. We are to ask regularly in prayer what we should be giving and to whom, and trust that the Lord will show us. We are to take Jesus' words on financial generosity sufficiently seriously that the question of what we should give away is never for a single day off our spiritual agenda.

Genuine humility helps us greatly with living a life of generosity because true humility does not desire the material things and the status that money brings. Humility enables us to put the desires of others before our own. Humility enables us to serve rather than wanting to have our way. Humility draws us into delighting in the rewards God gives others. Humility helps us not to compare but to focus instead on God's calling on our lives. When we live this way, God delights in our service and we can be assured that we will not lose our reward either – like all others, we will receive from God's generous hand blessings beyond anything we deserve.

1 Helper of the helpless

Matthew 20:29–34

This story follows on from Jesus' challenging teaching throughout chapters 18—19. In Matthew 18, Jesus calls his disciples to live as a community characterised by humility and mercy, where none claims status and all forgive whatever the cost. In Matthew 19, his teaching continues to call his disciples to holy living according to God's vision and commandments, giving ourselves for others just as Jesus gave himself for us. One could be forgiven for feeling quite helpless in the face of our vocation. But one of the key messages of Matthew is that Jesus does not leave us helpless but teaches us personally how to live as he calls (11:28–30). That Jesus helps us when we are helpless is the message of today's text.

Jesus leaves Jericho with a large crowd following him. Against all odds, two blind men seek Jesus for their healing. They have heard that he is coming their way. They can doubtless hear the size of the crowd and two people can easily go unnoticed in such a large crowd. They cannot see Jesus, so they can only call out for him. Their voices are easily drowned out by the many voices of the crowd. There are many obstacles in their way, but none of these stop them. They call out for Jesus: 'Have mercy on us, Lord, son of David' (v. 30). The crowd rebukes them, telling them to be silent, but this only makes them cry out all the more: 'Have mercy on us, Lord, Son of David' (v. 31). And then Jesus stands still and calls to them, asking them what they want him to do for them – 'Lord, let our eyes be opened' (v. 33). Jesus is overcome with compassion for them and heals their sight.

When overwhelmed, these men trusted Jesus. Three times they call him 'Lord'. They did not give up at the first hurdle but persisted in the hope that Jesus would hear their cry. Matthew pictures Jesus as the helper of the helpless, the one who has compassion on those who realise that their only hope is in him. He pictures Jesus as listening for those who call on him as Lord; and when we do so, he comes in compassion to heal us.

2 Jesus, son of David

This event is well-known, and its basic outline is familiar to many. Jesus enters Jerusalem on a donkey (and a colt in Matthew, see v. 7), fulfilling a prophecy about the Davidic king (Zechariah 9:9). The crowds greet him as the son of David. He enters Jerusalem as the messianic king but is rejected by the chief priests, scribes and (in Luke) leaders of the people. Each gospel writer shapes the story quite differently. So, we will focus on a detail that only Matthew includes, verse 14: 'The blind and lame came to him in the temple, and he cured them.'

We often hear that 'the son of David' refers to the messiah, the king who would rescue the Jews from Roman rule. This is partially right, but Jewish expectations of the messiah, or messiahs, were more complex and varied than that. For Matthew, Jesus' messiahship seems to have been manifested partly in his healing ministry. Matthew sees Jesus' healing of the crowds as a fulfilment of the prophecy of Isaiah 42:1–4. Just before Jesus enters Jerusalem, he heals two blind men who call on Jesus, as the 'son of David', to heal them (20:29–34). Unlike Mark and Luke, Matthew has the crowds cry out that Jesus is the 'son of David' (vv. 9, 15). An earlier son of David, namely Solomon, was associated with healing and exorcisms in Jewish culture during the centuries around the time of Jesus. Matthew picks up on this and presents Jesus' healing ministry as part of his work as messiah.

There may also be a hint of Jesus creating a new order here. Leviticus 21:18 did not permit the blind and the lame to offer sacrifices to God. Some Jewish groups around the time of Jesus reinforced this command (compare Mishnah Chagigah 1.1) or extended it so that the blind and lame were not permitted to join those entering God's coming kingdom (1QSa 2.6–9, one of the Dead Sea Scrolls). Jesus seems to take a different approach. He heals the blind and the lame, which means that nothing prevents them from enjoying the presence of God. Indeed, he heals all of us who are willing to be healed so that nothing can prevent us from enjoying the presence and love of God.

3 Some questions and possibilities

This text raises many questions: why did Jesus curse the fig tree? Why curse the tree if it was not the season for figs (compare Mark 11:13)? Does Jesus really expect his disciples to curse fruit trees that bear no fruit (v. 21)? Can faith really move mountains (v. 21)? It is easy to understand why interpreters commonly wonder whether we should seek a deeper meaning from this passage.

Possibly, Matthew intends us to understand what Mark does with this event. Mark shapes the whole event so we read Jesus cursing the fig tree as symbolic of Jesus pronouncing judgement on the temple. The Jewish leaders rejected Jesus as messiah and Jesus prophesies God's coming judgement on the nation for its sin and so calls it to repentance. He envisages God's judgement as the destruction of the temple. The tree having no figs is like the nation not having the fruits of righteousness and being unwilling to repent of its sins. When Jesus refers to 'this mountain' (v. 21), he is pointing to the temple mount in order to make all this clear. However, Matthew does not say so. He does not point any of these deeper meanings out. They are possible – just not as clearly there in the text.

In fact, Matthew seems to take the event in another direction. The punchline of this event in verse 22 has Jesus saying, 'Whatever you ask for in prayer with faith, you will receive.' Matthew wants us to take this seriously. He places this saying on the lips of Jesus. Matthew intended all those reading his gospel to take Jesus' words seriously. He stated that they would last for eternity (Matthew 24:35). So we should seek to pray in faith that God will answer. Many of us have experienced disappointment when things did not happen as we asked. They had the same struggles in the early church (compare James 4:2–3). James began to explore how we respond when the words of Jesus do not match our experience. I wish I had the answer, but I do not. So, I am simply going to recommend that we continue to call on the Lord, wrestling with him as we pray, trusting his timing, his faithfulness and his goodness.

5–11 June

47

4 Getting to the heart of the issue

Matthew 21:23–27

Sometimes we only hear half the argument. Some conversations are like that; the real issues do not actually make it into the words we say. Something like that is going on here. The chief priests and elders of the people do not want to ask themselves whether Jesus is the son of David. They get angry when they hear the crowds suggesting this in the temple (21:15). Nor does Matthew give us any indication that they want to respond in repentance to his call (compare 4:17). However, they clearly want to tackle Jesus. So, they ask Jesus where he gets his authority (v. 23).

Jesus gives them a straight answer. Rather than avoiding the question, he gets to the heart of the issue. Jesus' ministry begins with his call to repentance (4:17), which is the same as that of John the Baptist (3:2): 'Repent for the kingdom of heaven has drawn near.' Both Jesus and John called God's people to repent in the light of God's coming judgement on the nations. So, in asking the chief priests and elders of the people whether the baptism of John was from heaven or was of human origin, Jesus faces his questioners with the real issue. His ministry carried on the ministry of John, and so they would have to publicly put on record what they thought about John the Baptist. They did not want to do this for fear of the crowd, who regarded John the Baptist as a prophet. Insulting a martyred hero is a very dangerous thing. But Jesus' response is again not avoiding the issue. 'Neither am I telling you by what authority I do these things' (v. 27) gives a very clear answer, not just to the chief priests and the elders but to the crowds. The implication of the whole conversation is that Jesus continues the ministry of John the Baptist: calling the nations to repentance.

I write these words in the middle of Lent. Many wonderful people I know have given up chocolate again. Developing self-control is certainly a godly practice, but I do wonder whether sometimes we fail to look more deeply at what responding to Jesus' call to repentance in our lives might look like.

5 A short, sharp shock

Sometimes a short, sharp shock is precisely what we need. It is certainly what the chief priests and the elders of the people got in this parable. The meaning of the parable is beyond doubt as Jesus applies the story to the listeners. The man who had two sons is God. The chief priests and the elders of the people are the second son. They say they are willing to follow God but refuse to respond to God's call to repentance through John the Baptist. The first son represents notorious sinners: tax-collectors and prostitutes. They hear John calling them to repentance and respond by believing him. Consequently, they enter the kingdom of God ahead of the chief priests and elders. Jesus continues the response he made to them in the previous story – not only are you unwilling to answer my question about who gave John authority to minister, but you are also unwilling to respond to God's question through John: will you repent of your sins?

Jesus' challenge is shocking at all sorts of levels. Tax collectors practised extortion and worked with the Roman oppressors of the people. Prostitutes made a living out of breaking God's law and will for human sexuality – as well as, very likely, contributing to marital unfaithfulness and breakdown. To be told that people like this are close to God can have an emotional impact. Likewise, to suggest to people who have committed their lives to leading God's people that they have failed to hear God speak hits hard. Jesus' turning of the tables as he questioned them into a corner (which seems to have been what they were trying to do to him) must have been humiliating.

But surely this is the heart of the matter. They have status, authority and responsibility. John calls the whole nation to humility. Repentance entails humility as we cannot repent without admitting we have done badly, need the forgiveness of another and need to change the way we think and act. As we look at what the chief priests and elders of the people were so loath to do, we would do well to look at our own attitudes – particularly where we have status, authority or responsibility – and ensure that we are not above saying sorry for what we get wrong.

6 A very uncomfortable conversation

Matthew 21:33–46

I cannot imagine the tones of voice the chief priests and elders of the people must have used when they responded to Jesus that the owner of the vineyard would 'put those wretches to a miserable death, and lease the vineyard to other tenants who will give him the produce at the harvest time' (v. 41). Although Matthew notes in verse 45 that 'when the chief priests and Pharisees heard his parables, they realised that he was speaking about them', he has already indicated that they knew this as he has Jesus interpret the previous parable in a way which identified them as the disobedient son. So here they listen to this parable about a vineyard – doubtless recognising, from their knowledge of the scriptures, that the vineyard is Israel (compare Isaiah 5). The slaves sent to collect the produce would have sounded very much like God sending prophets to call back disobedient Israel, and then comes the climax when disobedient Israel kills God's Son.

At this point, Jesus ceases to tell the story and asks the chief priests and elders what happens next. Jesus has just identified them in his previous parable as the disobedient son who will not listen to the voice of God through the ministry of John the Baptist. Now, he asks them to tell him and the crowds what God will do with these disobedient people when he comes to judge. The emotional shock and public humiliation when Jesus asked them that question must have been great. Hence, I wonder what their tones of voice must have been and what kind of expressions they had on their faces.

Jesus goes on to tell the chief priests and elders of the people that the kingdom of God (the vineyard, Israel) will be taken away from them and given to another people who will act like God's people. Given the public nature and strength of his challenge, their desire to arrest him seems understandable. We would do well in our own churches and spiritual lives to regularly come before Jesus and ask him, by his Spirit, to show us where we go wrong and then come to him in repentance – turning away from all we do wrong and directing our lives down his paths, living as he teaches us.

Guidelines

The hostility between Jesus and the chief priests and elders has been building throughout most of this week's readings (Matthew 21:1–46). The chief priests and others begin with anger over Jesus' entry into Jerusalem and the temple, and they end wanting to arrest him. But before we assume this has all been one-sided, consider how Jesus responds to them. When challenged over the source of his authority, he returns the challenge and then builds on it in two parables. In the first, Jesus directly identifies the chief priests and those with them with the disobedient character in the parable and interprets this as their disobeying God by not responding to John the Baptist's call to repentance. Jesus takes this further in the next parable, where not only does he identify them as being responsible for the death of God's Son, but he also asks them what God would do with them by way of response.

There has been a tendency since the 1960s and 1970s to give Jesus a bit of a makeover – to make him the representative face of a Father God who longs to do nothing more than love us the way we want to be loved. Sometimes this is linked to a misinterpretation of the Aramaic word 'Abba' which, it is claimed, means 'Daddy'. But as the biblical scholar James Barr demonstrated in his famous article, 'Abba isn't daddy' (*Journal of Theological Studies* 39 [1988]: 28–47). Where we might be tempted to believe this contemporary narrative, stories like the ones we have been reading this week help to ground us back into fuller understanding of God as Father.

Jesus loves us just as the Father loves us. But this does not mean that Jesus has forgotten that he will come again to judge the living and the dead, or that through his ministry in the church today he calls us out of the sin we so love and into the lives of holiness God longs for us to live. In this ministry, Jesus remains prophetic. He calls us out when we disobey God – just as he did with the chief priests, elders and Pharisees. He calls us into renewed lives of justice, mercy, generosity and righteousness. Yes, Jesus loves us with the profoundest love, but he is not scared to challenge our sin.

1 A tale of two judgements

Matthew 22:1–14

The similar parable in Luke 14:16–24 ends at verse 10 of the parable here in Matthew, making some readers wonder whether Matthew has stuck two parables together. But this parable is a story of two wonderfully balanced halves which reflect each other remarkably closely: the king sends an invitation (vv. 3a, 8–9), the invited respond (vv. 3b, 10), the king speaks (vv. 4, 12a), the invited respond (vv. 5–6, 12b) and the king judges (vv. 7, 13). Topping and tailing Matthew's account are an introduction (v. 1) and a conclusion (v. 14). All this makes it look very much like Matthew intends the parable to read this way, but what is he doing?

Very likely, Matthew gives a panoramic view of God's plan to bring justice and to save in this parable. Matthew distinguishes between God's mission to Israel ('Go nowhere among the Gentiles … but go rather to the lost sheep of the house of Israel', Matthew 10:5) and God's mission to the Gentiles ('Go therefore and make disciples of all nations', Matthew 28:19). Matthew distinguishes between the judgement on Israel ('all the tribes of the earth [compare Zechariah 12:12–14] will mourn, and they will see the Son of Man coming', Matthew 24:30) and the judgement on the Gentile nations ('When the Son of Man comes in his glory… and all the nations will be gathered before him', Matthew 25:31–32). Just as Matthew has two mission invitations into the salvation of God in his gospel, so there are two invitations to the banquet of the king in this parable. Just as Matthew has two judgements in his gospel, so there are two judgements in this parable. As someone very much concerned for the Gentile mission, Matthew has God's plan for salvation for Israel and the Gentiles central to his gospel.

And that plan requires a response. As we wait for Jesus coming in glory, we wait like the wedding guests in the second half of the parable. The guests are expected to be dressed for the occasion. God longs to clothe us with robes of righteousness (compare Colossians 3:12–17). Today is the day of his gracious invitation. Let each of us respond by coming to his feast.

2 True corruption

At this point in Matthew's telling of Jesus' story, the Pharisees are understandably angry. Jesus has told one parable about God punishing them and handing the kingdom of God over to others (Matthew 21:33–41) and he has just told another parable implying God will destroy Jerusalem in punishment for their rejection of his gracious invitation to salvation (Matthew 22:1–14, especially v. 7). If we look at things from their point of view, we can see why they might plot to entrap him in his words.

So the Pharisees and the Herodians ask Jesus a double-edged question that touches on the important issues of faith. On the one side: do you want to fund a corrupt political order that oppresses God's people? Do you want to subvert the very salvation God won for his people in the exodus and the return from Babylonian exile by supporting the regime that makes us slaves and exiles in the land the Lord has given us? (After all, Jesus has told parables of the kingdom of God, and to many Jews this kingdom meant freedom and prosperity in the land that God had promised to Abraham.) And on the other side: do you want to oppose Rome in the name of freedom and risk what that entails? Do you want to be the reason hundreds more of God's people are killed by the Roman occupiers? You could probably have heard a pin drop as these were very real and very live questions of politics and faith.

Jesus' response is both simple and brilliant. Show me the coin used for the tax. They had no difficulty in finding one. In other words, they were already part of the corrupt system that some of them are egging him on to challenge. Jesus does not need to defend his record in standing up for God's kingdom vision. He simply lets the Pharisees' and Herodians' actions speak for themselves – that they are hypocrites who participate in the evil that they suggest Jesus challenge. Again, Jesus challenges people not simply to be hearers of his words but to be doers of his words. Jesus does not call us to have visions which we then tell others to live up to – he calls us to live out the vision God has already given us.

3 In the resurrection...

Today, I want to focus on the resurrection as there is enough to explore here without looking at the whole text – and we may find that Jesus' teaching astounds us as much as his first hearers. When people die, we often hear their loved ones talking about them going to heaven. If you read the gospels and count the times Jesus refers to life after death, you will find that Jesus hardly ever says anything about going to heaven when we die (although famously, his words to the thief on the cross in Luke 23:43 sound like this). Instead, Jesus shared, with some of his fellow Jews, the belief that there would come a day when God's people would rise from the dead and be judged. Some would go to eternal glory and others to eternal shame – a belief rooted in the hope of Daniel 12:1–3. There were various ideas of what eternal shame and glory looked like in Jewish texts (e.g. 4 Ezra and 1 Enoch), but Jesus did not necessarily believe the same as them as not all Jews at the time agreed on these things.

However, Matthew does give us a glimpse into Jesus' understanding, and I invite you to read the following passages from Matthew which will give you more of an idea of Jesus' understanding of resurrection. Jesus expected to judge all nations, sending some to eternal life and others to eternal punishment (25:31–46; compare 13:41–43). He expected those who had lived his teachings faithfully to be rewarded with honour in the kingdom (5:20; 7:21). He expected feasting (8:11; 26:29). He expected all who served God to be rewarded (10:40–42). Jesus spoke as if there would be society and justice in the kingdom (19:28–29; 20:20–23). Pondering these sayings, it sounds very much as if Jesus was expecting a new earth with a perfect society, social justice and celebration. This was very much the hope of the prophets (e.g. Isaiah 65:17–25). There is plenty more to say and explore as the subject of life after death in the New Testament is complex. But I would urge all of us to explore Jesus' vision carefully and take it to heart – it is our living hope!

4 The greatest commandment

Matthew 22:34–46

It is a strange thing that during the 20th century, Christians were largely responsible for misrepresenting Jesus in this and other texts like it. Inheriting their forefathers' reaction against Catholic ideas of earning merit to enter the kingdom of God, some Protestants have pitted law against love in their practical spirituality to the point where prominent Christians (like John Robinson and Joseph Fletcher) argued in the mid-20th century that discerning and following the way of love was the basic Christian ethic and that this could be sharply distinguished from any idea of discipleship through obedience to commands. Texts like today's have been used to suggest Jesus taught this idea.

Little could be further from the truth. Jesus is asked which is the greatest *commandment* in the *law*. Jesus answers with two *commandments* drawn from the *law*. The first, to love God with everything we are, comes from Deuteronomy 6:5. The second, to love our neighbours as ourselves, comes from Leviticus 19:18. Jesus gives a relatively straight answer to a straight question. He offers two commandments from the law, giving the greatest and adding the second most important. He then adds that the rest of the law, *and the prophets*, hang on these two commandments. In other words, we are to obey God's commandments, first through worship and second by loving others. This is quite the opposite of abandoning God's commandments to follow our personal sense of what love looks like. Interestingly, Jesus' addition of 'and the prophets' (v. 40) strongly implies that he expects God's people to live out the teaching of the prophets in addition to the commandments of the law. This is an even further cry from the strange idea of 20th-century 'spirituality' that love replaces the law.

I suspect the reason behind such ideas lies in the anti-authoritarian spirit of much of 20th-century western culture rather than the teaching of Jesus. Jesus was not afraid of the idea that God commands us to live worshipfully, lovingly and well. So, he taught us to do so. We do well to carefully question the spirit of our culture. We do even better to listen to Jesus' teachings and to live them out – after all, that is what we are committing ourselves to when we call him Lord.

5 Jesus the teacher

Jesus presents one of the most radical pictures of the church I have ever come across in verse 8 – and I love it: '*You* are not to be called rabbi, for you have one teacher, and you are all students.' It's worth filling in some historical detail. The disciples of Jewish rabbis would learn the Torah and the teachings of previous rabbis as the authoritative interpretation of the Torah as part of their training. Then they became rabbis who would continue the tradition of interpreting the law. They did so to help answer questions of how the commandments in the Torah applied to new situations, so that people knew in practical terms how to live out God's commands. Jesus makes the most astounding remark in verse 8 as he effectively stops this tradition in its tracks. Instead, he claims that he is the only rabbi and his is the only true interpretation of the law and one that will last forever (compare Matthew 24:34–35). He is the only interpreter of God's law, and we are all disciples who learn from him.

Although there are many giftings and ministries in the church, and some of these carry authority, Jesus' words create a radically equal status among his disciples. Even though Jesus commands the apostles to teach the nations all he had commanded them (Matthew 28:20a), they only do this through his empowering presence (Matthew 28:20b). In all that we each bring to the table of learning together in our congregations, we come humbly as those who all seek and need to learn from the one true teacher. In all we do in the teaching ministry in churches, none of us grow in understanding or spirituality except by the work of Jesus, our rabbi. All that Jesus has taught about the community of humility and mercy in Matthew 18 makes sense in the light of this declaration. We come as servants of each other (v. 11) rather than lording it over each other, for that will simply result in our being humbled (v. 12). We offer what gifts we have to each other, trusting that Jesus will use them to help us understand his ways better and to empower us to live them out both in our individual lives and as a community.

6 Learning from the Pharisees

Matthew 23:23–39

I remember starting one Ash Wednesday sermon with the line: 'I only wish I were half as righteous as the Pharisees.' It took the congregation by surprise, but I meant it. You see, we often take a passage like this one, read it quickly, maybe fail to find an encouraging message and so skip over it – gaining from our surface-reading of the text that the Pharisees were terrible people. I will not deny that passages like this make for difficult reading – not least for those of us who picture Jesus as unconditionally affirming of us in all our foibles and so 'on our side' that he never really challenges us. But that does not mean we have nothing to learn from this passage.

Take verses 23 and 24. The criticism is not that the Pharisees tithe their mint, dill and cumin. No, the rigorous way in which the Pharisees give a tenth of all they earn or grow is affirmed in Jesus' words 'without neglecting the others'. Now this is where the challenge starts. The Pharisees are criticised for neglecting the weightier matters of the law: 'justice, mercy and faith' (v. 23). Take justice. The biblical vision of justice (which Luke makes much of in Luke and Acts) includes radical financial generosity on the part of Christian disciples at personal cost to themselves (e.g. Acts 4:32–35). Possibly some of the Christian Pharisees (compare Acts 15:5) were among those who gave so sacrificially. Now we need to compare ourselves to the Pharisees in the light of Jesus' vision of justice. How many of us give over and above our tithe to share our goods with the poor? The huge disparity between our incomes in wealthy countries like the UK and those of many of our brothers and sisters in the majority world puts our ideas of 'low income' into a sobering global perspective. How many of us actually tithe our income? Asking questions like these can help us to see that the Pharisees are doing quite well compared to many of us. Through hearing Jesus' challenge to them, we can hear his challenge to us and begin to pray for the courage and strength to step out into the active faith Jesus wants to grow in all his disciples.

Guidelines

This week's readings have been of intensifying disputes and some criticisms which are really quite hard to hear – and yet, in recording these events in Jesus' life and the things he said, Matthew invites us to hear the challenging side of Jesus, one which can be quite difficult to come to terms with for many today.

In many Christian traditions today, I suspect that the teaching Jesus has largely been replaced by the therapeutic Jesus. The Matthean and Marcan picture of Jesus both begin with Jesus calling people to repentance. He identifies us as sinners who stand to be judged by God and so are not worthy of life in the kingdom. His mission is to call us to repentance, forgive our sins and teach us how to turn our lives around – and he gives us the strength to do this. (This is also clear in Luke and present in John, but they start their gospels with different emphases.) As Jesus calls people to repentance, he also heals them and delivers them from evil powers. Contemporary reflections on the gospels often focus on Jesus' healings and try to reframe the story in the light of them – making Jesus' healing ministry central and letting the ethical challenge (call to repentance, forgiveness and changed lives) drop down the agenda. As much as Luke does frame his gospel in terms of Jesus healing individuals and society (see his summary of Jesus' mission in Luke 4:18–19), Luke never lets the challenge to repentance and changed lives fall from the picture. Indeed, he keeps the challenge to accept or reject Jesus as a central theme right to the end of Acts. But somewhere along the line, I suspect that many of us have taken the therapeutic Jesus from Luke and allowed the ethical Jesus to fall out of our direct line of vision.

This might help to explain why Jesus' challenges are so difficult to read. We cannot see how our therapeutic Jesus is binding up people's wounds. In fact, he might seem to be wounding people with his words. But the Jesus of the gospels can only be read rightly when we realise how straight-talking he is, and we need to allow this insight to shape our spiritual lives and our prayers.

FURTHER READING

Andy Angel, *The Jesus You Really Didn't Know: Rediscovering the teaching ministry of Jesus* (Cascade, 2019).

R.T. France, *The Gospel of Matthew* (Eerdmans, 2007).

N.T. Wright, *Surprised by Hope: Rethinking heaven, the resurrection and the mission of the church* (SPCK, 2011).

Refugees and the Bible

Rosie Button

This week of notes has been timed to fall in Refugee Month. World Refugee Day is on 20 June (**UNHCR, see unhcr.org/uk/world-refugee-day.html**) and the nearest Sunday is recognised by many churches as Refugee Sunday: a time when refugees are honoured and their plight highlighted. At the time of writing, there are an estimated 89 million refugees across the world (**unhcr. org/uk/figures-at-a-glance.html**) including at the moment many thousands of Ukrainians. The number of people in Britain who have opened their homes to Ukrainian families is heart-warming. It seems it should be a non-issue that Christians would welcome, love and seek to help refugees, yet sometimes this statement is viewed as controversial. The so-called 'refugee crisis' is a complex topic which has sadly, but perhaps inevitably, been politicised. But what does the Bible say about refugees, and does it have anything to say about a Christian response? In this week's Bible readings, we will look at passages which speak into this – both directly and indirectly.

The well-known parable of the good Samaritan (Luke 10:25–37) is a power-ful lesson in loving our neighbour. Jesus calls us not to be like the priest and the Levite who walked by on the other side, but to emulate the Samaritan, the unlikely hero of the story – an outsider himself – who stopped and helped a person in trouble. The injured man was a stranger to him, and supposedly his political enemy, yet the Samaritan saw him as a neighbour whom he could help and went out of his way to do so. This would be one obvious place to start. Another would be Jesus' teaching in Matthew 25:31–46: 'For I was hungry and you gave me something to eat, I was thirsty and you gave me something to drink, I was a stranger and you invited me in' (v. 35). Whatever we do to welcome and show love and hospitality to refugees, we do to him. An honour, surely; but is it a nice 'added extra' – or a must of Christian living?

Starting in the Pentateuch with God's instructions to his covenant people to welcome the foreigner in their midst, this week we will look at passages throughout the Bible that show us God's heart for refugees.

Unless otherwise stated, Bible quotations are taken from the NIV.

1 Love the foreigner as your own

Deuteronomy 24:10–22; 26:1–11

In Deuteronomy, Moses' final words to the Israelites remind them of the law and guidance given by God at Sinai, in preparation for beginning life as a nation in the land of Canaan. Although they are to understand that they are God's unique, special people, who should therefore live differently than the nations around them, this was not supposed to mean they should be exclusive and inhospitable. On the contrary, God had told them in Leviticus 19:34: 'The foreigner residing among you must be treated as your native-born. Love them as yourself, for you were foreigners in Egypt.'

Commands about loving orphans, widows and aliens occur 92 times in the Old Testament. The Hebrew word translated by the NIV as 'foreigner' is *ger*, which means foreigner, stranger, sojourner, temporary resident, resident alien or immigrant. Refugees in various ways fit these descriptions. God's people are told to treat the *ger* as one of their own, as kin.

In today's verses, Moses illustrates how they are to do this. Deuteronomy 24:12–15 talks about showing simple, decent justice and kindness to people in need and insists that the foreigner is to be treated with this same fairness as a fellow Israelite. Verses 19–21 show that they are to share their excess with those in need: especially foreigners, orphans and widows. In other words, they are to regard the sojourners among them as being the same as their own people in need who had no family to provide for them. While gleaning is not a practice we use today, we can think of modern equivalents; it doesn't mean giving away our rubbish (think, worn-out clothes), but of using only the resources we need (whether money or time) and being generous with the rest.

In 26:11 the Israelites were told to include the foreigners with them in their festival, in essence to treat them as members of their community and households. This was countercultural. But God wanted his people to draw the outsiders in, to love them as their own and give them a home and community to belong to. As motivation, they are reminded that they themselves had been homeless as a people, more than once (vv. 5–9), and God had given them homes and provision: they should be willing to pass on this blessing. This injunction, to demonstrate in these ways the heart of God for wanderers, is surely just as relevant for us today.

2 He led them to a city where they could settle

Psalm 107:1–17, 23–32, 43

This beautiful psalm shows us God's heart for the lost, the scared, the hungry and the homeless. Think for a moment: who are the wandering people in this psalm? Is it remembering when the Israelites were wandering in the wilderness after fleeing Egypt? Or is it when the Jews had been scattered in exile from their homeland and God brought them back?

There are four different scenarios in the psalm. It seems most likely it was written after the return from the Babylonian exile, celebrating that, but not only referring to that specific event in the history of the Jewish people. Rather, a range of situations, not necessarily about the whole people of Israel, are described: in verses 2–3 some were rescued from an enemy, being gathered from east, west, north and south; in verse 4 some wandered in desert wastelands, finding no city to settle in; in verses 5 and 10 some were thirsty and hungry or in utter darkness; in verse 23–25 some set out on the sea as merchants but became lost and endangered when a storm arose. In each case, God rescued them, provided for them and brought them to a safe place. Metaphors perhaps for God's response to people who are lost and afraid and in need of a haven.

Significantly, notice that verses 10–14 and verse 17 suggest that the people in these scenarios brought their suffering upon themselves, yet still when they cried out to God, his heart was for them and he saved them. It hardly needs saying, I don't mean this is true of refugees. But notice, God doesn't save the people in this psalm because they deserved it, or because they were innocent sufferers. He rescues them because of his compassion and love; when they cry out to him, he responds. I have heard people sometimes say about refugees, 'they shouldn't have left their own countries,' or 'they knew it would be dangerous to get here', as if their situation was their own fault. Would that be God's response to them? No, this psalm shows us that God's desire for us humans is to have what we call 'home': a safe haven (v. 30). He satisfies the thirsty and fills the hungry with good things (v. 9). As God's people, Christians are his body here on earth. Do we have this same heart for those who come among us? Are we being his hands and feet to them?

3 The God who sees

Genesis 16:1–14; 21:9–19

Today's verses continue the theme of God's heart for the homeless and rejected, in a surprisingly powerful story full of twists and turns. In many ways, the narrative in the first section you read has so much awfulness in it, describing a messy family situation where nobody behaves well. But Hagar ends up being the victim, fleeing the home (v. 6) having lost the protection of Abram by whom she is pregnant. (Note that Hagar would have had no say in any of this, as a foreign slave.) But the angel of the Lord found Hagar in the desert and asked her, 'Where have you come from, and where are you going?' (v. 8) Even though Hagar's pregnancy was outside of God's plan for Israel, even though she was 'surplus to requirements', even though her pregnancy was the result of Sarai and Abram's impatience and lack of trust in God's promise, even though Hagar herself had been guilty of a bit of pride… God didn't let her flee unnoticed into the desert to die. He found her, approached her and spoke to her: 'Where have you come from, and where are you going?' He is the 'God who sees'. Hagar says, 'You are the God who sees me… I have now seen the One who sees me' (v. 13). I find this awesome in the true sense of the word. God sees us, even when nobody else does. God sees refugees when they are alone, rejected, on the road and fleeing for their lives. Do we?

The second section of the Hagar narrative, in chapter 21, tells how Hagar was once again ejected from the home, this time after Ishmael and Isaac were born. Again she finds herself in the desert and facing death, the death of her son. God did not abandon her this time either: he kept an eye on her, spoke to her again, gave her hope for her and her son's future and provided the water she needed to survive.

This is not to say that God rescues every single refugee. Clearly, he doesn't, just as he doesn't heal every sick person. But this story gives us an incredibly intimate insight into God's heart for a rejected woman and mother in desperate trouble. How did he view her? What did he do? How should we respond?

4 Refuge under God's wings

Ruth 1:1-22, 2:11-12

The book of Ruth tells of two movements of people across borders. It starts with the story of Elimelek's family, who were forced to leave Judah because of famine, becoming what we would today call economic migrants, moving to Moab (Glanville in *Refuge Reimagined* calls them 'survival migrants', p. 60). They settled in and their sons married local girls there. Years later, the second movement happened, when after all three men of the family had died, Naomi returned home with her Moabite daughter-in-law, Ruth. Picture these two brave women arriving in Bethlehem. Naomi is an elderly widow and returnee who has lost everything; as she herself expresses it, 'The Lord has brought me back empty' (v. 21). Ruth is a foreigner who has left behind all her blood relations, familiar home culture and religion. They are starting from scratch, at the bottom of the heap. I imagine this is how many refugees feel.

The gleaning rule mentioned in our Deuteronomy reading from three days ago helps them, as Ruth is allowed to work in the fields of Boaz, who is from Elimelek's clan. Ruth's hard work is noticed. Boaz gives her his protection, but also prays God's blessing on her in 2:12: 'May you be richly rewarded by the Lord, the God of Israel, under whose wings you have come to take refuge.' It is a beautiful image of God's wings extending to cover and draw in an outsider who is in need of a home. As we know, eventually their marriage ensues and Ruth, the impoverished, once-widowed migrant, enters the heart of salvation history, as the great-grandmother of David and an ancestor of Jesus.

Obviously, Ruth's story and its outcome is unique and very special! But the underlying truths are there for us to learn from. Those who seek refuge in God, as Ruth did, will be embraced and blessed by him. Refugees are not outside of God's plans; he has a role in his kingdom for every one of us who believe. Welcoming refugees might start with obedience to Christian principles, but often leads to wonderful bonds of friendship and fellowship where we become family. Let's be encouraged to be God's blessing to refugees, and let's pray that many will become believers – maybe even through our welcome and the friendships we make.

5 God's plan for the nations

At the beginning of Acts, we read Jesus' well-known commissioning of the disciples: 'You will be my witnesses… to the ends of the earth' (1:8). The section for today from chapter 17 is a classic example of Paul carrying this out, in a contextualised way, to the philosophers of Athens. It is a model for us of reaching non-Christians with the gospel, by meeting them on familiar territory (the altar 'to an unknown god' in their case) and going on to explain how our God is the one true creator God and the true fulfilment of all religious belief.

Verses 26 to 28 are especially intriguing for us thinking about refugees, when you picture Paul in the cross-cultural setting he was in: a Jewish travelling preacher in the heart of the cultured Greek philosophical world. First, he says that we are all descended from one man (Adam). Then he states that it is God who planned the times and boundaries of the nations, with the purpose that all peoples in every nation should seek him and somehow come to know him. Then he points out that God is actually not far from any of us, no matter where we are in the world.

This all might raise a few questions, but for the sake of this short reflection, there are key points that speak into our topic. First, it is a great reminder that although we are from different cultures, possibly dressing, eating and interacting differently from one another, we are all one family and all created by the same God who longs for us all to know him. Second, God is close to refugees: where they came from and on their journeys, and he is with them now, as he is with us.

On the one hand, refugees coming to live in our neighbourhood gives us an opportunity to share the gospel 'with the nations', so to speak, to obey Jesus' commission, so that people may hear the gospel who might otherwise not have in their homeland. And on the other hand, just as often, refugees come to us as Christians who bring a new, fresh and vibrant faith to enrich our churches. We are certainly seeing both these things happening in churches in my hometown and it is very exciting. God has a plan for the nations and he is using the refugee situation to further it: hallelujah!

6 Welcome the stranger

Romans 12:1–16

This chapter spells out how we should live in light of the truths about God just described ('Oh, the depths of the riches of the wisdom and knowledge of God!', Romans 11:33–36). In worshipful response, we are to give over our lives in every way, not acting as the world does, but counterculturally, in obedience to God's will.

We are urged to live as one body, each contributing our particular gifts (vv. 4–8). Universal commands follow (vv. 9–16): we are to show one another love, care and support. And we are told to 'practise hospitality'. (This same command is given to Timothy and Titus as essential aspects of their roles as church leaders; compare 1 Timothy 3:2 and Titus 1:8.) We can misunderstand this word in British culture, thinking of it as inviting some friends for dinner, or keeping the spare room clean just in case. But the New Testament word is diametrically different, *philoxenia*, meaning 'love of stranger (or foreigner)', with the opposite meaning to xenophobia. Opening our hearts and homes to friends is one thing, but doing so to strangers takes a bolder step of faith, openness and love.

Frequently, when we were missionaries, we were welcomed in and fed generously by people who barely knew us, whether in Uganda where hospitality is an extremely high value and the words 'You are welcome!' are often heard, or on church visits in our home countries. Gratitude, comfort and relief were engendered in me as the recipient: it was such a tangible sign of love and being part of the body of Christ. Matthew Soerens in the foreword to Glanville and Glanville's *Refuge Reimagined* says, 'When we welcome strangers well, they do not remain strangers: we quickly recognise them as neighbours and ultimately embrace them as part of us' (p. ix).

Philoxenia is a perfect picture of welcoming refugees and making them our friends. The instructions in verse 15, to rejoice with those who rejoice and weep with those who weep, is a beautiful picture of the solidarity and oneness which God wants us to have with those we are living alongside. In my hometown, there is a wonderful community 'World Café' (now called 'Unity Community') where local Christians befriend and share meals with refugees and other immigrants in the area: they truly do rejoice and mourn alongside each other, and close friendships are made. It is an inspiring example of hospitality.

Guidelines:

I hope this week of Bible readings has inspired you to engage with the people living among us who need our welcome, hospitality and friendship.

In these kinds of conversations, it is often said as the clinching argument, 'Jesus was a refugee!' But why does that mean we should help refugees? You could spend some time considering that question.

We have also seen this week how God loves refugees, desires us all to have a home and has repeatedly given refugees a place in his plan of salvation. We have thought about Hagar and Ruth, but in the Bible there are many people who are refugees. Many had to flee persecution from governments who wanted to do them harm. The nation of Judah was deported en masse. God provided in different ways in their times of desperate need.

You could look up some of their stories and review how God provided for them in their journeys and worked through the events of their lives. Does reading their stories through the lens of refugees teach you anything more about how God views refugees, and what response God might be asking you to make to the Bible readings this week?

Conclude this week by spending time in prayer for refugees. Spend a few minutes praying for the following categories: those who have fled from war; those who as Christians have fled from religious persecution; those who have lost children or other family members along the way; those who have settled in your home area, that they might find the welcome and haven they need. Also pray for the work of refugee settlement agencies, and pray for governments to have wisdom and compassion in making decisions on behalf of their nations regarding people seeking refuge there.

FURTHER READING

Samuel George and Miriam Adeney (eds.), *Refugee Diaspora: Missions amid the greatest humanitarian crisis of the world* (William Carey Publishers, 2018).

Mark R. Glanville and Luke Glanville, *Refuge Reimagined: Biblical kinship in global politics* (IVP, 2021).

Krish Kandiah, *God is Stranger: Finding God in unexpected places* (Hodder & Stoughton, 2017).

The Centre for Mission Mobilisation, Xplore: 'Welcoming the Nations among us: engaging with your cross-cultural neighbours for the sake of the gospel' (**resources@mobilization.org**), 2019.

Joel, Obadiah, Micah, Zephaniah

Alison Lo

These two coming weeks are focusing on four books of the minor prophets –
Joel, Obadiah, Micah and Zephaniah.

The date of Joel's ministry is uncertain, though the setting in Judah and the
temple worship in Jerusalem indicate that it is not exilic. His addressees are
Judah and Jerusalem. Despite its canonical location between the two eighth-
century prophets (Hosea and Amos), a relatively late date (i.e. post-exilic) for
Joel is generally supported because it parallels a number of other books, which
may hint a dependence on them. Joel tells of a locust plague, which will attack
Israel on the day of the Lord. He thus urges the Israelites to repent.

Obadiah addresses Edom and Judah. The prophet declares that the Edomites
will face God's judgement as they join the Babylonians capturing and plunder-
ing their brother Israelites when Babylon destroys Jerusalem (586BC). So the
setting of Obadiah's ministry is exilic.

The eighth-century prophet Micah addresses the southern kingdom. He
warns Judah to learn the lesson from the fall of the northern kingdom and urges
them to return to God before it is too late. In face of the moral, religious and
political corruption, Micah teaches his people what is a true believer – doing
justice, loving kindness and walking humbly with God (Micah 6:8).

Zephaniah is a seventh-century prophet, who addresses Judah. Judah's
corruptions (religious, economic, moral and leadership) rouse God's wrath.
The day of the Lord will come imminently and God will sweep away everything
from the whole earth. Zephaniah urges the people of Judah to repent before
the universal judgement arrives.

Unless otherwise stated, quotations are from the NRSV.

1 Locust and drought

Joel 1:1–20

Joel warns about the imminence of the day of the Lord. When it comes, God's people will suffer locust infestation (vv. 1–4). Though it is difficult to specify the four different terms for locusts – the cutting locust, the swarming locust, the hopping locust and the destroying locust – the four consecutive attacks by different kinds of locust probably symbolise a complete destruction by this plague (v. 4). In addition to this natural disaster, Joel also prophesies a severe drought which will soon hit the land (vv. 19–20). How terrible is the day of the Lord? Joel describes the plight as follows: first, the food will be cut off (v. 16a); second, joy and gladness from the temple will disappear (v. 16b); third, the storehouses will be desolate due to poor harvest (v. 17); fourth, the animals groan because there is no water and pasture (v. 18).

Due to the severity of the pending judgement from God, the prophet urges his people to wail and mourn. It is noteworthy that four groups from the community are summoned by Joel. But why are the drunkards and all the wine-drinkers first addressed (vv. 5–7)? In the ancient Near East, drinking wine is their daily custom. Therefore, Joel does not simply target the drunkards, but the people of the whole nation, as everyone drinks wine (v. 5). The wine-drinkers will be first hit hard when the locust attack the vines and fig trees because their fruits are the ingredients for winemaking (vv. 6–7).

The second group of people is not specified. They are summoned to lament as though they were a virgin mourning for the death of her engaged husband (v. 8). The desolation caused by the locust also affects the temple as grain offering and drink offering are cut off. Even the priests mourn about the situation (vv. 9–10).

Third, farmers and vinedressers are urged to wail (vv. 11–12) as all the crops of the field are ruined by the locust. Finally, the priests are asked to put on sackcloth because grain offering and drink offering are held off (vv. 13, 9–10). They need to lead their people as follows (v. 14): sanctify a fast; call a solemn assembly; gather the elders and all the inhabitants to the temple; cry out to the Lord for deliverance. To sum up, all walks of life are hit hard when the day of the Lord comes.

2 Who are the invaders?

There is no consensus regarding who the 'invaders' are in the book of Joel. Are they referring to the locust plague, an army of human warriors or eschatological situations in the end time? Let's first take a look at the first two perspectives.

The vivid descriptions of the locust can be found in many places in Joel. For instance, there are four attacks by the locust (1:4; 2:25); they strip off the bark of the vines and fig trees (1:7); after them the land becomes a desolate wilderness and nothing escapes them (2:3); they leap upon the city, they run upon the walls (2:9); the sun and the moon are darkened, and the stars withdraw their shining (2:10); they have the appearance of horses, and they charge like war-horses (2:4); as with the rumbling of chariots, they leap on the tops of mountains, like the crackling of the fire flame they devour the stubble, like a powerful army they are drawn up for battle (2:5); God sends the swarming locust, the hopper, the destroyer and the cutter to punish his people (2:25). It doesn't make sense if they are not referring to the locust.

But then in other places, a human army is brought to the scenes. Joel announces that a nation invades his land (1:6) and a great and powerful army comes (2:2). The jargons of warfare and the depiction of an army's invasion are frequently seen in 2:2b–11. For example, 'horses', 'war-horses' (2:4); the rumbling of chariots, a powerful army drawn up for battle (2:5); warriors... charge, soldiers... scale the wall... they do not swerve from their paths (2:7); they burst through the weapons (2:8); the Lord utters his voice at the head of his army (2:11). If the locust is not pointing to the invading army, God's promise to remove 'the northern army' in 2:20 would not make sense. Since locusts are compared to armies elsewhere in the Old Testament (compare Judges 6:5; 7:12; Nahum 3:15–16; Jeremiah 46:23; 51:14), we should not deny the possibility of interpreting the locust as an army. Actually, one will find it difficult to differentiate whether it is locust or army in 1:6 and 2:2b–9 – the locust is likened to an army and vice versa. Joel most probably refers to the invasion of both locust and army, which simply witnesses God as the Lord of nature and human history.

3 Eschatological phenomena

The last note ended with a conclusion that the 'invader' could be both 'locust' and 'army'. Now let's take a look at the third perspective – eschatological phenomena. Alongside the description of the locust and army, there is no lack of eschatological jargon, which closely links with other passages in the book. For instance, when the attack of the locust is depicted, Joel proclaims that 'the day of the Lord is near, and as destruction from the Almighty it comes' (1:15). When the army is described, Joel's message carries a strong eschatological sense: 'Let all the inhabitants of the land tremble, for the day of the Lord is coming, it is near – a day of darkness and gloom, a day of clouds and thick darkness!' (2:1–2). Such expression is intensified in 2:10, where 'the earth quakes before them, the heavens tremble. The sun and the moon are darkened, and the stars withdraw their shining.'

This focus on the day of the Lord is further developed throughout the rest of the book. God promises that when he comes to judge the nations on the great and terrible day of the Lord, he will save those Israelites who trust in him (2:32). Before this day comes, God will show warning signs in the heavens and on the earth, blood and fire and columns of smoke (2:30). The sun shall be turned to darkness, and the moon to blood (2:31). This theme not only echoes 2:10, but also flows into 3:14–16. When God judges all the nations on the day of the Lord, multitudes and multitudes are gathered at the valley of Jehoshaphat (3:14). Relentlessly similar eschatological phenomena appear here again: 'The sun and the moon are darkened, and the stars withdraw their shining' (3:15; compare 2:10). A warfare between God-sent warriors and all the nations is predicted in this context (3:9–11). Since the prophetic message may have multiple fulfilments in different times and spaces, we cannot rule out the possibility that locust and army in Joel 1—2 may ultimately refer to the eschatological army in the end time.

4 Duties of brotherhood

Edom's proudest achievements are revealed in the text. First, located on the mountains of Seir, the Edomites built their cities on the rocky cliffs and lived in well-defended high caves, which gave them a strong sense of superiority and security as though they were eagles nesting among the stars (vv. 3–4). Second, Edom gained diplomatic support by making alliance with other nations (v. 7). Third, the Edomites were so wealthy that they hid their treasures in the mountain caves (v. 6). Fourth, Teman (a city representing Edom) was known for its wisdom (compare Jeremiah 49:7; Baruch 3:22–23). Job's wise friend Eliphaz was a Temanite (Job 2:11). There was no lack of human resources in Edom – the wise men (v. 8) and mighty warriors (v. 9). Its strategic location, international support, great wealth and talented people led to Edom's arrogance and complacency.

'Pride goes before destruction, and a haughty spirit before a fall' (Proverbs 16:18). Obadiah prophesied that Edom would be humiliated and destroyed. Despite its natural defence in high mountains, God brought Edom down from its great height (v. 4). Their treasures and possessions were completely searched out and plundered (vv. 5–6). Its international alliance was simply a false security as the Edomites were betrayed and deceived by their allies (v.7). God would destroy their wise men (v. 8) and scatter all their warriors (v. 9).

Why did Obadiah prophesy the total destruction of Edom? When Judah was invaded by the Babylonians, far from supporting their brothers, the people of Edom committed horrendous crimes against the Israelites. The Edomites joined the Babylonians to plunder Jerusalem (vv. 10–11, 13). They even rejoiced over the misfortune of Judah on the day of distress (v. 12) and helped Israel's enemies capture Jewish refugees (v. 14). Verses 10–14 help locate the historical timeframe for Obadiah's message, that is, Judah's fall to Babylon in 586BC. There is a general consensus among biblical scholars over this historical backdrop, which is supported by many other texts in the Old Testament (Psalm 137:7; Lamentations 4:18–22; Ezekiel 25:12–14; 35:1–15).

5 Obadiah's link with Joel and Amos

Obadiah's judgement oracles are beyond doubt directed to Edom. Edom refers not simply to one nation, but also represents those nations who rebel against God. As Obadiah made clear, the day of the Lord is near against all the nations, which will be judged according to what they have done (vv. 15–16). However, the judgment against Edom (vv. 1–14) and all the nations (vv. 15–16) reflects only one side of the day of the Lord. Regarding the other side, God has promised to restore Judah. Its survivors will repossess the properties and territory that were lost to their enemies (vv. 17b, 19–20). They will cut off the Edomites (v. 18). Mount Zion will be a holy mountain where the remnant shall be (vv. 17a, 21a). Finally, God will establish his kingdom (v. 21).

Located right after the books of Joel and Amos, Obadiah is the fourth of the minor prophets, and shares many similarities with its immediate predecessors. The book of Amos concludes with God's promise to restore Israel, where Amos prophesies, 'On that day I will raise up the booth of David that is fallen, and repair its breaches, and raise up its ruins, and rebuild it as in the days of old; in order that **they may possess the remnant of Edom** and all the nations who are called by my name, says the Lord who does this' (Amos 9:11–12). Juxtaposed right after Amos, Obadiah seems to give Amos 9:12, 'they may possess the remnant of Edom', an interpretation.

It is noteworthy that Joel 3:19 clearly points out that 'Egypt shall become a desolation and **Edom a desolate wilderness, because of the violence done to the people of Judah, in whose land they have shed innocent blood**'. Whereas Obadiah 15–21 helps interpret Amos 9:12, Obadiah 1–14 gives further details about the violence Edom did to the people of Judah in Joel 3:19. The examples above demonstrate the close relationship between Joel, Amos and Obadiah.

6 Diversity and unity

The book of Micah demonstrates a very tight structure, which comprises three rounds of messages. Each message contains a proclamation of judgement and a promise of deliverance as follows. First round of message: proclamation of judgement (1:1—2:11) and promise of restoration (2:12-13). Second round of message: proclamation of judgement (3:1—12) and promise of restoration (4:1—5:15). Third round of message: proclamation of judgement (6:1—7:7) and promise of restoration (7:8-20).

Each round of message starts with an imperative 'Hear/Listen' (1:2; 3:1; 6:1). Although Joel's prophecy of judgement targets the people in Judah and Jerusalem, he does not disclose and criticise their sins. Micah is the first book of the minor prophets making direct and strong criticisms against the sins of Judah and Jerusalem. So it is special that the remnant theme of Micah follows the thematic thread of Amos (points 1–4 below) and flowing from Micah it opens up close linkage with Zephaniah from a new perspective (points 4–6 below):

1 After God's judgement upon Judah and Jerusalem, a remnant will survive (Micah 5:7-8; Amos 9:8). They will triumph over their enemies (Micah 5:9; 7:16; Amos 9:12). Their boundary shall be far extended (Micah 7:11; Amos 9:12).

2 God will restore the Davidic kingdom (Micah 5:2–5a; Amos 9:11). The remnant shall live secure under the new king (Micah 5:4–5a; Amos 9:15).

3 God will rebuild Jerusalem and cities in Judah (Micah 7:11-12; Amos 9:11, 14).

4 God will bring the remnant back to the promised land (Micah 4:6–7; Amos 9:14; Zephaniah 3:19-20).

5 God will fight against the enemies on behalf of Judah (Micah 7:14-17; Zephaniah 3:14-17).

6 God will uplift the remnant and make them a strong nation. He will reign over them in Zion forever (Micah 4:6–7; Zephaniah 3:19-20).

To sum up, like any of the other minor prophets, the book of Micah can be studied as an individual book, which conveys a special message to a particular audience. Yet it can also be read alongside other minor prophets as they share some common themes in the collection. Importantly, interpreting the minor prophets should take into consideration both the diversity and unity represented.

Guidelines

When earthquake, tsunami, hurricane, flood, drought, wildfire, plague, etc. happen, modern people tend to see these as natural phenomena and try to explain them from a scientific perspective. God's acts behind these disasters are hardly taken into consideration. Of course, we should refrain from going to an extreme that all natural disasters are attributed to God's judgement against human sins. However, Joel reminds us that ecological crisis and natural disasters sometimes have close ties with human sin. Joel 1:10 clearly points out, 'The fields are devastated, the ground mourns.' When people fall, nature becomes anguished too, just as Paul puts it, 'the whole creation has been groaning in labour pains until now' (Romans 8:22). May natural disasters remind us that God is the Lord of nature and he is our fair judge.

In the past when God acted to deliver the Israelites, he reminded them to pass on God's deeds to their next generations, for example the Israelites' exodus from Egypt (Exodus 10:2; 13:8) and God's helping the Israelites cross the Jordan (Joshua 4:20–24). These are triumphant examples to share. It is surprising to find out that Joel urges his people to tell their next generations about God's judgement against his people through the locust plague (Joel 1:3). When people give testimony, most of them tend to share their success stories, not to boldly tell people about their failure before the Lord. Actually, God's discipline for our wrong deeds powerfully helps others to see God's mercy and grace upon us. It helps cultivate a culture of honesty, sincerity and vulnerability in the community.

When Obadiah condemns the Edomites' pride and arrogance, some people may not consider it so much a problem. Living in a highly materialistic and competitive world, many contemporary people, including Christians, are pursuing the same things as the Edomites. We are urged to climb up the social ladder, break records and be the 'number one' in terms of fame, wealth and power. May the Edomites' failure and destruction open our blind eyes to see these problems, which take us away from God.

1 Function of wordplay

Micah 2:1–11

Due to God's impending judgment upon Judah, just as happened to Israel (1:2–7), Micah mourns for his nation's upcoming fatal calamity by uttering a dirge (1:8–16). What on earth has Judah done to deserve such a punishment? Here Micah singles out two groups of people for their wrongdoings. Those who covet others' fields and properties are first to be blamed. They 'devise' evil deeds on their beds and perform them when the morning dawns (2:1–2). Ironically, God is 'devising' against these evil people that they cannot escape from the yoke of being captives. God will let the captors remove the land from these wicked people. In the land allocation for the assembly of the Lord, those who covet others' fields will have no offspring to inherit the land. What is interesting is that God retaliates the evil the same way as they treat others (2:3–5).

The second group to be denounced are those who stop Micah and his colleagues from prophesying unpopular messages about God's judgement (2:6–7). Micah further discloses their evil deeds. They 'rise up' against their own people as an enemy, stripping the robe from those peace-lovers (2:8). They deprive the women and their children of their pleasant houses and God's blessings (2:9). Now God commands them to 'rise' and go into exile (2:10), just as Moses warns that when people sin, they not only defile themselves, but they also defile the land, which will in return vomit them out for defiling it (Leviticus 18:24–28). These people only love to hear the prosperity gospel ('wine and strong drink') from the false prophets (2:11), but not the unpleasant message from Micah (2:6).

The puns and wordplays in this passage are eye-catching. The first pair appears to be 'devise' (בשׁח; 2:1, 3) while the second pair is 'rise up' (מוק; 2:8, 10). The use of these two pairs of verbs serves to remind us of God's role as the fair judge, who pays back justly the evil deeds of the evil-doers.

2 Ideal kingdom of God

Micah's second round of message contains a judgement oracle against the leaders (Micah 3) and a promise of restoration to Judah (Micah 4—5). Micah 3 discloses the sins of the political and religious leaders. The heads and rulers act like a butcher, slaughtering their people (3:1–4). They pervert justice and equity, building Jerusalem with blood and wrong (3:9–10). They give judgement for a bribe (3:11a). The false prophets lead people astray. They preach good news when they are fed but declare war against people if they are not (3:5–8). The priests teach for a price and the prophets give oracles for money (3:11b). This oracle vividly illustrates the corruption of leadership in Judah.

Interestingly, the promise of restoration in Micah 4—5 seems to resolve the leadership issues in Micah 3 by establishing an ideal kingdom of God. First, Zion will become an international centre, where peoples from all nations will stream in to learn God's words. God will bring universal peace among the nations (4:1–4). Second, God will bring the remnant to their homeland and make them a strong nation. Restoring their former dominion, God will reign over them in Mount Zion forever (4:6–7). Third, God will raise up an ideal king among his people. This king comes forth from Bethlehem of Ephrathah, and his origin is from of old, from ancient days. By the strength and the name of the Lord, he will shepherd his flock so that they may live securely. He shall be the one of peace (5:2–5).

Micah's prophecy was fulfilled literally about 700 years later in the birth of Jesus. Bethlehem was a royal city, where David was born (Ruth 4:11, 21–22; 1 Samuel 16:18; 17:12). Despite its seeming insignificance, God chose Bethlehem Ephrathah as the birthplace of King David and the natal home of Jesus (Matthew 2:1, 5–6; Luke 2:4, 11). Wonderful is the providence of the sovereign God, who moved Caesar Augustus to decree a census that made Joseph and Mary travel from Nazareth to Bethlehem, where Jesus was born according to Micah's proclamation (Luke 2:1–7; Micah 5:2). This ideal kingdom established by Jesus is already here but not yet complete.

3 Who is a God like you?

The author of Micah reveals the sins of Judah and Jerusalem throughout this book. But nothing is as shocking as the descriptions in Micah 7:1–6:

- In Judah there is no one faithful and upright left in the land (7:2a).
- Everyone is lying in wait for murder, and they hunt each other with nets (7:2b).
- They are skilled to do evil. The official and the judge ask for a bribe. The powerful do what they desire and they pervert justice (7:3).
- The best of them and the most upright of them are like a briar and a thorn hedge respectively. They are useless (7:4a), but waiting for their punishment to come (7:4b).
- People will not trust in one another, including friends and loved ones. Even someone as intimate as a wife cannot be trusted (7:5).
- The family is so broken that the son treats his father with contempt, the daughter rises up against her mother, the daughter-in-law against her mother-in-law. Sadly, their enemies are the members of their household (7:6).

From the government, to neighbours, to friends and family, every single unit is full of greed, suspicion and hostility. Social disintegration and moral decay are seen everywhere. Just as after the summer harvest there is no fruit left in the orchard, no one faithful and righteous can be found in Judah (7:1).

The character of God strongly contrasts with the nature of his people. The book concludes with Micah's marvel, 'Who is a God like you?' The prophet is amazed by God's mercy in pardoning iniquity and passing over his people's transgression. He does not retain his anger as he delights in showing his grace (7:18). His compassion is clearly shown as he treads his people's iniquities under foot and casts all their sins into the depth of the sea (7:19). After all, God faithfully keeps his promise made to Abraham and Jacob (7:20). It is no coincidence that the prophet's question 'Who is a God like you?' echoes his own name 'Micah' (meaning 'Who is like the Lord?'), thus constantly reminding us of God's character.

4 The day of the Lord

'The day of the Lord' appears three times in the book of Zephaniah (1:7, 8, 14). Various descriptions of this day can be found throughout the book. For example, 'the great day of the Lord' (1:14); 'the day of the Lord's wrath' (1:18; 2:2, 3); 'a day of wrath' (1:15); 'a day of distress and anguish' (1:15); 'a day of ruin and devastation' (1:15); 'a day of darkness and gloom' (1:15); 'a day of clouds and thick darkness' (1:15); 'a day of trumpet blast and battle' (1:16); 'on that day' (1:9–10; 3:11, 16); 'at that time' (1:12; 3:9, 19–20), etc. This long list of repeated terms indicates that 'the day of the Lord' is the key theme of Zephaniah.

Zephaniah 1:2–3, 18 and 3:8 point out that when the day of the Lord comes, God's judgement will be universal. He will utterly sweep away everything from the face of the earth, including humans, animals, birds, fish and so on. His wrath will come upon Judah (1:4–18) and all the nations (2:4–15). Apart from the just side of God, the book of Zephaniah also underscores the heart of God's mercy and compassion. After the judgement, God will reserve a humble and faithful 'remnant' (2:7, 9; 3:9–10, 12–13). On that day, all the nations will gather together to worship the Lord (2:11; 3:9–10, 12–13). This fully expresses that the Lord is not only the God of Israel, but also the God of all nations.

The author of Zephaniah uses *inclusio* to highlight the key theme and structure of the book. Zephaniah 1:2–3 introduces God's universal judgement, 'I will utterly sweep away everything from the face of the earth'. This theme is repeated in 1:18 and concluded in 3:8, 'In the fire of [his] passion all the earth shall be consumed.' Zephaniah 3:8 serves as the watershed, which divides the whole book into two parts. The first section (1:1—3:8) highlights the universal judgement on the day of the Lord, whereas the second section (3:9–20) depicts God's salvation and comfort to Israel and all nations on the day of the Lord.

5 Oracles against Judah and all nations

Both Judah and the nations are held accountable for the disasters on the day of the Lord. About Judah, Zephaniah makes the following points:

Religious adultery rouses God's wrath (1:4–6). Some people worship false gods and idols such as Baal (1:4). Some practise syncretism: bowing to Yahweh, but also worshipping false gods, such as the host of the heavens (1:5a) and Milcom (1:5c). Others turn away from the Lord and do not seek him (1:6).

Leadership corruption raises the alarm (1:7–9). God will punish the officials, royal family and those who wear the attire of idolatrous priests (1:8). He will also bring judgement to those who practise 'leaping over the threshold' at the temple of Dagon (1:9a; compare 1 Samuel 5:5). .

Complacency plagues God's people (1:10–13). Market districts and commercial places like the Fish Gate and Second Quarter will be attacked by God (1:10). All the merchants and traders who practise fraud will perish (1:11). These people 'rest complacently' and they think God will not act (1:12). In the end, their wealth will be plundered and their houses laid waste (1:13).

All nations are responsible for impending calamity on the day of the Lord as well (2:4–15):

- **The west (2:4–7):** Gaza, Ashkelon, Ashdod and Ekron on the west coast will be desolated (2:4). These once prosperous cities will become pasture for shepherd and flocks (2:6), and they will become dwelling places of the Jewish remnant (2:7).

- **The east (2:8–11):** God will deal with Moabites and Ammonites in the east, who scoffed, taunted and boasted against God's people (2:8, 10). The remnant of God's people will take possession of their land (2:9).

- **The south (2:12):** The next target is the Ethiopians in the south, who will be killed by God's sword.

- **The north (2:13–15):** Finally, God will destroy Assyria (2:13–14). When they invade Israel, they go along the River Euphrates up to the north of Palestine, from where they head down to attack Israel. That's why Assyria is considered an enemy in the north. Other peoples scoff over Assyria's ruin and desolation (2:15).

These neighbouring countries do not exhaust the list, but they powerfully symbolise 'all the nations'. It demonstrates that God is the fair judge of the whole earth.

6 God rejoices with us?

The restoration message in the second section of Zephaniah (3:9–20) is full of hope and comfort. Among all, 3:14–17 gives a most impressive illustration. Zephaniah exhorts the people of Jerusalem and all Israel to sing aloud, to shout, to rejoice and exult with all their hearts (3:14). Why? The prophet points out some reasons for jubilation and great celebration. First, it is because God has taken away the judgements against the Israelites, and he has turned away their enemies (3:15a). Second, the king of Israel, the Lord, is in their midst, and thus they will never again fear evil (3:15b). Third, the people of Jerusalem shall not fear and their hands will grow strong (3:16).

It is not surprising to see these people rejoice, particularly when they deeply experience God's grace and deliverance. There is no lack of scripture depicting people's jubilation. However, God's response to his people in 3:17 is so extraordinary that nowhere in the Bible makes the same description. We all know that the Lord, Israel's God, is in their midst, and he is a divine warrior who gives victory (3:17a; 3:15b). But what is amazing is that God will rejoice over his people with gladness (3:17b)! 'He will be quiet in his love' (3:17c; NASB), which means that when God quietly ponders about his people, he cannot hold his deep love for them within him. Eventually his silence bursts into jubilation. He will exult over his people with loud singing (3:17d). We can hardly imagine how God sings when he rejoices over the Israelites.

There is a sense of echo between 3:14 and 3:17 – Zephaniah's exhortation to sing aloud and rejoice parallel to God's acts of rejoicing and loud singing. The intimate love of God for his children is vividly revealed.

Guidelines

Micah must be very depressed when he declares that no one faithful and righteous can be found in Judah. Every unit in that society is full of greed, suspicion, and hostility (7:1–6). Why is the prophet able to sing praise at the end (7:18–20)? It is because God is an incomparable God. Micah proclaims on an upbeat note: 'Who is a God like you, pardoning iniquity and passing over the transgression of the remnant of your possession? He does not retain his anger forever, because he delights in showing clemency' (7:18). What makes God incomparable? First, God forgives sins out of his compassion. Second, he does not retain his anger forever. Third, he is able to overcome and remove sins completely. Micah is confident that God is able to deal with his people's sins.

Micah discloses the corruption of the religious leaders. Leading people astray, the false prophets preach good news when they are fed or they will declare war against people (3:5). Therefore, they don't get any vision, revelation and answer from God (3:6–7). Contrary to these false prophets, Micah declares, 'But as for me, I am filled with power, with the spirit of the Lord, and with justice and might, to declare to Jacob his transgression and to Israel his sin' (3:8). When every unit of the society is completely disintegrated and everyone morally decayed (7:1–6), Micah declares his faith, 'But as for me, I will look to the Lord, I will wait for the God of my salvation; my God will hear me' (7:7). No wonder this 'one in a million' prophet is mightily used and blessed by God because of his utmost faithfulness.

Many Christians often focus on the God in the New Testament as a loving God (seen in fullness in the sacrifice of Christ) but tend to forget about the fearfulness and justice of God. Some even take God's forgiveness and compassion for granted, and they continue to sin against God. However, Zephaniah mentions repeatedly that God's wrath pours out against his sinful people (1:15, 18; 2:1–3, etc.). This reminds us that God is a just and fearful God. We need to revere him in great awe.

FURTHER READING

Allen, L.C. *The Books of Joel, Obadiah, Jonah and Micah* (NICOT) (Eerdmans, 1976).

Nogalski, J.D. *The Book of the Twelve: Hosea – Jonah* (Smyth & Helwys Bible Commentary) (Smyth & Helwys Publishing, 2011).

Nogalski, J.D. *The Book of the Twelve: Micah – Malachi* (Smyth & Helwys Bible Commentary) (Smyth & Helwys Publishing, 2011).

Robertson, O.P. *The Books of Nahum, Habakkuk and Zephaniah* (NICOT) (Eerdmans, 1990).

Smith, R.L. *Micah – Malachi* (WBC) (Word Books, 1984).

Stuart, D. *Hosea – Jonah* (WBC (Word Books, 1987).

Sweeney, M.A. *The Twelve Prophets: Hosea, Joel, Amos, Obadiah, Jonah* (Berit Olam. Vol.1) (Liturgical Press, 2000).

Sweeney, M.A. *The Twelve Prophets: Micah, Nahum, Habakkuk, Zephaniah, Haggai, Zechariah, Malachi* (Berit Olam. Vol. 2) (Liturgical Press, 2000).

A typology of shame

Sally Nash

When was the last time you experienced shame? While it is a disputed concept in some ways, there is broad agreement across disciplines that shame is about who we are – that is, it impacts our sense of self – whereas guilt relates to what we have done. We may feel either or both about the same incident. Some of us are more shame-prone than others and it is a culturally contextual concept. Synonyms for the verb 'to shame' include defile, dishonour, debase, discredit, humiliate, mortify, ridicule, smear and stain. Not experiences I would choose to either go through or inflict on others! Being shamed can lead to feeling, for example, worthless, flawed, unlovable, inferior, exposed, defective or helpless.

My interest in shame was the focus of the academic element of my ordination training. Having been badly shamed by school as an eight-year-old, I had a lingering mistrust of institutions as shaming places. In getting ordained, I was keen to be a minister who was shame-aware and did not intentionally or inadvertently act in such a way that people experienced disgrace or shame through my inappropriate words or actions. As part of this, I devised a typology of shame in the church and will explore each of the six elements in these notes.

It is important to acknowledge that shame is not only negative. There is such a thing as healthy shame, which is around boundaries, identity, intimacy, modesty and dignity, and the Holy Spirit may convict us in a way where we experience shame or guilt or both. I did not research this element, sometimes known as discretion shame, and instead focused on disgrace shame.

The Bible was written in cultural contexts which saw shame and the associated concept of honour through a collectivist rather than individualistic lens. They are important missiological concepts, with many majority world cultures also taking a more collectivist perspective, and understanding shame can bring insights to our mission and ministry. I will focus on six passages from Luke's gospel in exploring my typology of shame.

Unless otherwise stated, Bible quotations are taken from the NRSV.

1 Personal shame

Luke 6:17–26

Feeling shame because of poverty is an experience growing numbers of people can resonate with in challenging economic times. The first beatitude or makarism (transliteration of the Greek) says, more bluntly in Luke than Matthew, 'Blessed are you who are poor' (v. 20). The Greek word used is *ptōchos*, which means the very poorest, those worn down by poverty, beggars, the destitute.

Commentators such as Neyrey (1998) argue that the terms 'blessed' and 'woe' used in some translations can be rendered 'honoured' and 'shamed'. Thus, in this passage Jesus suggests that those who in the cultural context of the time are shamed can be seen as honoured: a turnaround of values that we find elsewhere in the teaching of Jesus (e.g. Matthew 20:16). Honour in New Testament times was a public attribute denoting value and worth, something which might be acquired or lost. Had Jesus not turned water into wine at the wedding in Cana (John 2:1–11), the family would have been shamed for failing to demonstrate expected standards of hospitality.

Personal shame in my typology is that which is experienced because of involvement with the church. Luke's fourth makarism, 'Blessed are you when people hate you, and when they exclude you, revile you, and defame you on account of the Son of Man' (v. 22), is true for some who make a decision to follow Jesus and as a consequence end up cut off from family and friends. While that is an extreme faced by some, others may experience shame from rejection or mocking by those who do not like our decision, for many different reasons.

However, my research highlighted that the church still sometimes operates out of cultural rather than biblical values and that people felt shamed by church members and leaders over things ranging from tattoos, living in the wrong part of town, being a single parent, accent, literacy levels and many other things which seem to be in opposition to the idea that 'honoured are the poor'. I continually look for opportunities to honour people and to seek to mediate the values Jesus demonstrates in this passage, honouring those who might expect to be shamed. The gospel is for all, especially those who may have experienced shaming.

2 Communal shame

Shame is sometimes used in a communal setting to do one of at least three things: control behaviour through shaming any breaking of cultural norms or mores; manipulate social status so certain attributes, achievements or possessions are given greater honour; and maintain social cohesion through excluding those who do not fit or belong. Communal shame often involves stigmatising groups of people as well as individuals and, in my typology, is what occurs at a group or congregation level.

The parable of the friend at midnight can be seen through a shame lens. There are two aspects of this. First, the hospitality conventions of the day would mean that if a visitor turned up, and in this case, they may have been travelling a long while, you offered food. To have no food available would be shameful. Guests should be treated with honour and fed. However, in the New Testament context, the shame is not individualised; it would be shaming for the community – hence the persistence of the friend repeatedly asking for help. The word translated 'persistence' in the Greek in the NRSV, *anaideia*, might also be translated 'shamelessness'. For someone not to get up to fulfil their obligation of hospitality could be seen as shameless, so even if you do not want to get up for the friend, you should be willing to uphold the honour of your community, particularly given that if you do not you would be the focus of gossip the next day!

This parable helps us to see that sometimes cultural conventions can be used to shame us into behaving in the way that the majority deem appropriate. We may want to reflect if there are occasions when this is unhelpful or if there are cultural conventions normalised in our context which are in fact not biblical.

Those listening to Jesus would have understood well the shame dimension of this parable and how much more honourable God is than the reluctant friend. The parable comes in the midst of a discourse on prayer, which includes what we know as the Lord's Prayer and encouragement to persevere in prayer, petitioning God in the light of an understanding of his goodness.

3 Vicarious shame

Luke 22:31–34, 54–62

Vicarious shame is what is experienced because of identification (by self or others) with the words, actions or behaviour of another or others in the church. In my typology, I am particularly connecting it to identification with leaders.

While I think Peter experienced personal shame after the cock crowed and he was reminded of the words of Jesus, 'I tell you, Peter, the cock will not crow this day, until you have denied three times that you know me' (v. 34), I also think he experienced vicarious shame when confronted by the servant girl and another person. For Peter to admit to the servant girl that he was one of the followers of Jesus would have meant a loss of face, a core experience of shame. He may have felt tainted by his association with Jesus; taint is a common occurrence with shame. With two people addressing him, Peter was beginning to experience a communal public shaming because of his connection to Jesus.

Vicarious shame is something that we might experience ourselves because of our association with the church. One of my research respondents commented that 'it is often the voices I hear representing the church that bring me the most shame', and this was reflected in different ways across theological traditions. It is significant because it impacts our identity and sometimes leads to us withdrawing from the institution that we associate with the vicarious shame experienced. Perhaps that also contributed to Peter going back to fishing after the incidents in our Bible readings. Withdrawing felt like the safer or more comfortable option.

Depending on our cultural context, we might experience vicarious shame in everyday engagements with people because we think they may make assumptions about our beliefs or have expectations of us because we are a Christian. Shame is deemed to always have an audience and we can experience vicarious shame because of how we think our audience perceives that part of the church we are associated with. This can inhibit our witness and it is helpful to be mindful of the concept of vicarious shame and look to mitigate its impact on our lives.

4 Structural shame

Luke 5:12–26

Structural shame occurs as a result of what the church says at an institutional level. The first section of our passage today is subtitled in my Bible 'Jesus cleanses a leper' and the second 'Jesus heals a paralytic'. We read in Leviticus 13:45 that 'the person who has the leprous disease shall wear torn clothes and let the hair of his head be dishevelled; and he shall cover his upper lip and cry out "Unclean, unclean."' If an animal touched a leper, it had to be killed; if they entered a house it had to be burnt. Lepers were untouchable and their leprosy was sometimes seen as a sign of sin, exacerbating their shame and rejection.

The passage describes the person as covered with leprosy, his condition and associated shame at being unclean, which would be obvious to all. Commentators tend to agree that leprosy is used as a term to encompass a range of skin diseases, including psoriasis, which is still prevalent today. In the gospels, there is a dissonance between how Jesus approached people who were outsiders or unclean and the official position mediated by religious leaders. Jesus touched the leper; that would have evoked astonishment in the crowd. The Greek word *hēpsato*, which is translated 'touch', more properly means 'to attach oneself to'; some speculate that this may mean something more akin to an embrace. For someone who may not have been touched by anyone for many years, imagine how liberating and healing this would be. Jesus completes the healing and encourages the necessary ritual attached to this.

The last line of our passage is: 'We have seen strange things today.' Jesus acted positively towards those others shunned – both the leper and the paralytic here – often healing and restoring them to be part of society. Once a person no longer had leprosy, they could rejoin the community (Leviticus 13:46).

For many years I have interviewed people for ministry training. I lost count of the number of people who in essence said to me, 'I am not sure you will accept me; I am a single parent, divorced, have no qualifications, have been in prison…' In essence they thought we might have policies that designated them 'unclean'. This led me to reflect on who the Jesus or God we are worshipping is. Is there anything about how we operate at a structural level which means people would think they are not welcome?

5 Theological shame

Theological shame relates to institutional belief systems and the way in which our theological beliefs can engender shame. In my Bible, today's reading is titled 'A sinful woman forgiven' and the person hosting Jesus, Simon the Pharisee, is dismayed at what she does and the way Jesus reacts to her. Again, we see that Jesus engaged with touching and being touched in a culturally dissonant way.

The Greek word used to describe the woman as a sinner is *hamartolos*. It is the same word Peter uses of himself in Luke 5:8 as Jesus calls him to be a disciple. Reflecting on both uses of the word may help us appreciate that, despite feelings of sinfulness, we can both approach Jesus as the woman did and respond to the call of Jesus as Peter did. Theological beliefs about our worthiness, value, etc. should not hold us back from coming to Jesus. We need his perspective on our shame and to understand his love for us and acceptance of us.

At the heart of this passage and some theological shame is the concept of purity. The Pharisees focused on the purity of the physical and social body and largely saw pollution as an external thing, thus the actions of the woman in our passage polluted Jesus. Jesus' response to the woman shows how he has a different approach. Jesus sees what comes out of the heart and it is that which might hurt the social body and which is impure.

When purity guidelines exist, disgust is often present in those who seek to enforce the guidelines. When we are looked upon with disgust, this is likely to cause us shame and some of it occurs through deeply held theological beliefs. For some people, this means that they may seek to hide parts of themselves which they think are deemed shameful from the church. Jesus' response to the woman, and his rebuke of Simon for his treatment of him with a lack of dignity and culturally gracious hospitable practices, demonstrates the importance of welcoming all who want to come and encounter Jesus.

6 Historical shame

Luke 1:26–45

Historical or buried shame in my typology relates to something which has happened in the past but still has an impact on current church life. It is often not spoken about, but you can see or sense the impact of a historical action and wonder what causes this. Individually or corporately, we might bear an emotional burden from the past which requires resolving.

I wonder what whispers there were about Mary and her pregnancy. I wonder if things were said to and about Jesus concerning his start in life. Some suggest that the response of Jesus to the woman caught in adultery (John 8:1–11) may have been influenced by his own history, knowing what might have happened to his mother had Joseph responded differently.

Our Bible reading today talks about Mary who 'went with haste' (v. 39) to her cousin Elizabeth, perhaps looking for sanctuary after shocking news and wanting a trusted person to explore a myriad of feelings with. The angel had told Mary that Elizabeth was pregnant (v. 36) and it must have been reassuring for Mary to arrive and see that this part of what the angel had said was true. Elizabeth responded prophetically to Mary, blessing her and acknowledging the message of the angel (vv. 42–45). Elizabeth provided a safe space, empathy, a refuge for Mary, and it was after her encounter with Elizabeth that Mary sang her song of praise that we know as the Magnificat.

This response of Elizabeth to Mary is likely to have mitigated the shame Mary could have felt. Even knowing what the angel had said to her, she may well have had to cope with murmurings and snide comments over the years.

We sometimes carry baggage from our past which can be alleviated when people know about and understand it. Some of this baggage carries shame with it, which needs processing. Imposter syndrome is something many of us face at different times, and we need people like Elizabeth to speak the truth to us as to how God sees us and to affirm our calling. Honouring, loving, accepting and journeying with someone are ways to help people through imposter syndrome and the hidden shame that can be felt in many situations.

Guidelines

Shame can be very difficult to recognise and admit to because of the impact on our identity and self-perception. The wonderful news of the gospel is that Jesus 'willingly gives up status and honour, to the point of death, in order to include the excluded and honour the shamed' (Georges and Baker, 2016, p. 10). As Hebrews 12:2 notes, Jesus 'endured the cross, disregarding its shame, and has taken his seat at the right hand of the throne of God'. Pattison thus argues that 'in this community of redefined honour and shame, healing miracles, epiphanies and other signs confirm God's reign has begun' (2013, p. 105).

Sadly, despite what Jesus has accomplished on the cross, we can still experience shame in a variety of ways in our engagement with the church, as I have explored over this week of readings. There are two challenges to this. First, reflecting on our engagement with people and seeking to avoid shaming them. Second, offering acceptance and affirmation and walking alongside people, helping them to belong and to experience the love of God, as they process shame.

FURTHER READING

Simon Cozens, *Looking Shame in the Eye: A path to understanding grace and freedom* (IVP, 2019).

Jayson Georges, Mark D. Baker, *Ministering in Honor-Shame Cultures: Biblical foundations and practical essentials* (IVP, 2016).

Sally Nash, *Shame and the Church: Exploring and transforming practice* (SCM, 2020).

Jerome H. Neyrey, *Honor and Shame in the Gospel of Matthew* (Westminster John Knox, 1998).

Stephen Pattison, *Shame: Theory, therapy, theology* (Cambridge University Press, 2000).

Stephen Pattison, *Saving Face: Enfacement, shame, theology* (Ashgate, 2013).

Judith Rossall, *Forbidden Fruit and Fig Leaves: Reading the Bible with the shamed* (SCM, 2020).

Robin Stockitt, *Restoring the Shamed: Towards a theology of shame* (Cascade, 2012).

Romans 9—12: rolling with Romans

Stephen Finamore

Paul has reached a turning point in his letter. He has set out his case that, through Messiah Jesus, God is keeping his ancient promise that one day he would put the world back on track. Paul has reminded his readers about what had gone wrong and how it affected every part of humankind. Our disobedience had derailed us so that we were unable to be what we were intended to be when God first created us. Even the Jewish people, those who had God's law, were not immune to this. In fact, the law, the possession of which defined the Jewish people, clarified the underlying issue – Paul calls it sin – by holding it up to the light. Furthermore, the law itself was conflicted and this led, in its turn, to a conflict in the very being of those who tried to live under the law's authority.

Paul has shown that the great problem of sin has been resolved through Messiah Jesus and by the gift of God's Spirit to his people. God's people have been put back on to the right track and they now form the vanguard that will lead to the renewal of the whole created order. God is completely committed to keeping his promises and therefore those who belong to God through Jesus can be assured that nothing can separate them from God's love.

These promises are made to the renewed people of God who are drawn from both Jews and Gentiles. Inevitably, this raises a couple of questions in Paul's mind. First, where do the Jews, or more specifically, those of them who have not believed in Messiah Jesus, fit into the plan? Or to put it another way, since the promises were given to Israel, what part does Israel play in God's continuing purposes? In one sense, to speak of the Jews and to speak of Israel is to use two different names for the same group of people. However, Paul uses the name *Israel* to speak of God's people as a collective whole and as the group to whom God has made covenant promises. Paul's second question, given all that he has argued, is how should the Christians in Rome live in response to what God has done? That is, what general and specific ethical guidance flows from the things Paul has taught up to this point?

Unless otherwise stated, scripture references are taken from the ESV.

1 Facing the facts

Romans 9:1–5

Paul turns to the most pressing question. The promises, which are the great theme of his letter, were given to Israel, so what part would Israel play in God's ongoing plans? For the most part, Israel had not accepted Jesus as the Messiah. They do not believe that he is the one through whom God is keeping his promises. Is it possible, then, that God's word had failed? The question was a very real one for Paul and he found himself in great anguish. Paul would happily be rejected by God himself if it would mean the acceptance by God of his fellow Israelites. They are Paul's ethnic family, the ones who share the same line of descent. Paul calls them his family 'according to the flesh' (v. 3). And this kind of relationship really matters. Many of the great things God has done are for them and many of his great gifts belong to them. Paul carefully does not call them Jews at this point, with its connotations, at the time, of politics and nationality and links to land. Instead, he talks about Israel, the name drawn from the Hebrew scriptures, the name that reflects the people's spiritual heritage. Israel is the name Paul uses to describe the covenant people of God as a collective group.

This people group is deeply honoured. Israel is God's son and her kings, as representative figures, bore this title, hence the idea of adoption. In addition, everything associated with the tabernacle and the temple, with the law and God's covenant promises belongs to Israel. The Messiah himself is an ethnic Israelite. All these things lead Paul to question what God seemed to be doing.

2 The two ways of understanding Israel

Romans 9:6–18

All the promises belong to Israel, yet when God fulfilled those promises, many within Israel did not believe it. It might look as though something has gone badly wrong, but in fact, God has been true to his word and consistent in his pattern of dealing with his people. Paul argues, and this is the beginning of his answer to his own question, that there are – and have always been – two ways to understand Israel. Abraham has both physical and spiritual descendants and the two groups overlap but are not identical. God has always distinguished between Israel according to the flesh and Israel according to the promise. We might call them genetic Israel and spiritual Israel. For example, Isaac was chosen over Ishmael and Jacob was chosen over Esau. It is for God to decide which category people are in.

This may sound arbitrary, but Paul's point is that ethnic descent is never a guarantee of God's favour and is not something that should ever be relied on as a basis for belonging to God. If you read the story of the people of God in the Hebrew scriptures, then this becomes clear. And this is not true of ethnic Israelites alone – the same thing applies to others, as the example of Pharaoh makes clear. It is a matter for God to decide when and where he be merciful. He determines who does and who does not belong to his spiritual people.

3 The potter and the clay

Romans 9:19–33

At this point, Paul introduces one of his imaginary dialogue partners. This one wonders how God can be a fair judge when he's the one making all the decisions. The apostle's response is based on the prophecies of Isaiah (29:16) and Jeremiah (18:1–11). Isaiah argues that the clay used by a potter can't tell the potter that the potter doesn't know what he's doing. One's the artist and the other's just raw material. Jeremiah insists that, just as a potter may rework the clay he is using, so God may rework both Israel and the surrounding nations according to his own purposes. Out of the same clay, the potter may craft something precious for use on special occasions or a bin to put rubbish in – things to treasure or things to throw away. We should note that Jeremiah makes it clear that this all happens in response to Israel's conduct, and this may be in Paul's mind as he writes.

Paul speaks again of God's wrath and the underlying metaphor is of God as a judge who is motivated to act in ways that achieve justice. God acts on behalf of his people and this group, Paul explains, based on prophetic promises in Hosea, consists of both Jews and non-Jews. In addition, Paul insists that Isaiah has shown that God has sometimes allowed the spiritual component within ethnic Israel to be reduced to a small fraction of the nation as a whole. He is implying that something similar is happening in his own day.

Paul then asks how this has come about. His answer is that non-Jews, that is those who had never sought to live as God originally intended, have arrived, on the basis of faith, at a place where they have begun to live that way. He is talking about Gentile Christians. Ethnic Israel, on the other hand, *did* seek to live as God intended but they sought to do it, not on the basis of faith, but on the basis of the Torah and, as a people, they never managed to fully live it out. Their problem was that, collectively, they didn't seek to live God's way on the basis of trust in God but on the basis of works – badges of their ethnic identity. The result of this approach is that they failed to recognise their Messiah when he came – just as Isaiah had prophesied – and so have stumbled on their journey with God.

4 Where Israel took a wrong turn

Romans 10:1–4

Paul makes it clear that he is distressed by the things he sees happening to ethnic Israel. He takes no pleasure in their current predicament. He longs for them to find their way back to God. It's not that they lack a desire for God but that they are going about things in the wrong way. God has given a way that enables people to live as God intended, but ethnic Israel is trying to reach that goal in a different way, and it doesn't work. They have not grasped the fact that God is already fulfilling his ancient promises. When the Messiah came, the law's purpose was fulfilled, it had done its job. From that point on, living in God's way is something that is available on the basis of trust and faith in the death and resurrection of Jesus and of loyalty to God.

5 Two sides to the law

Romans 10:5–13

Here, Paul seems to return to the idea of a conflicted Torah. He explores that split through two different quotations. If you are seeking to live as God intended based on obedience to the Torah, then you are believing that it's the doing of things that will bring you life. On the other hand, the law acknowledges a way to live as God intended that comes through faith. It doesn't depend on our efforts to achieve what God has promised – to climb into the heights or out of the depths. Instead, this is something that depends on words we can speak aloud because they spring from what God has done in our hearts, that is in our inner lives. The action of God within us giving us faith in and loyalty towards himself, the one who raised Jesus from the dead, finds expression in our acknowledging publicly that Jesus is Lord. This faith commitment makes us a part of God's people and therefore a part of the group who will find favour in the final judgement. Jesus, the very same person who's coming has caused ethnic Israel to stumble, is the one in whom those who belong to God put their trust. And this is true whether we are Jews or non-Jews, because the one God is God of all the world and of all people. Indeed, as the scripture promises, everyone (whoever they are and wherever they're from, be they Jew or Gentile) who calls on him will be saved.

6 The call to proclaim

Romans 10.14 – 21

This is the reason we have missionaries and evangelists sent out by churches to tell everyone what God has done. Before people can call on the true God, they must be able to offer him their trust and loyalty. And they can't do that unless they've heard about him, which means that someone must let people know about him. That's why churches, directed by God's Spirit, send people out. It's a wonderful thing and it's celebrated in one of Isaiah's prophecies. However, sadly, not everyone who hears the message responds to it in faith. Some do not believe. The point is that faith cannot emerge at all unless people hear the message, and that message is all about what God has done and is doing through Messiah Jesus.

Paul then asks whether there are any who have not heard? He is speaking about ethnic Israel in particular. He says there are none because the ones who are proclaiming the message are going out into the whole world. However, though it may have heard, ethnic Israel as a whole has not grasped what God is up to. It's just as Moses predicted, ethnic Israel is becoming jealous of and angry with a people – the Gentiles who have believed the gospel – who are not even a nation. This is confirmed by Isaiah when he prophesies about a time when people – and Paul is talking about the Gentile believers – find God even though they were not seeking him. Sadly, God's word to ethnic Israel at that time is that he has pleaded with them, in spite of their disobedience, but to no avail.

Guidelines

Paul is following the trail of his own argument, drawing on the pain of his own experience, his knowledge of the scriptures and his understanding of the impact of the gospel on the people called Israel. Like one of the many Hebrew prophets who felt called to proclaim something that was true to God but who seemed traitors to their own people, Paul sets out what God's plans will mean for the nation that was embraced by his covenant and his law. However things may seem, God has been true to his covenant, has kept his promises and has been consistent with the story of his past dealings with Israel.

- People have different understandings of Romans 9—11. The understanding that is true must be consistent with Paul's words in 9:3, where he admits to great sorrow and unceasing anguish with respect to his own people. What might this imply?

- How helpful is it that Paul speaks of two different understandings of Israel – one 'spiritual' and one 'genetic'. Does this suggest anything to those who feel they belong to a 'Christian' nation, whether Britain, the USA or holy Russia?

- Paul speaks of the rights of a potter over the clay they use and compares this to God and people. How helpful is this analogy? Does it strike you as helpful or as offensive?

- Jesus speaks of fulfilling the law (Matthew 5:17) and Paul argues that love is the fulfilling of the law (Romans 13:10). Are these things at odds with the insistence that Christ is the end/goal of the law as stated at 10:4?

1 The 'remnant' as a pattern in Israel's story

Romans 11:1–12

If ethnic Israel has become disobedient, this might be understood to mean that God has rejected them completely. Paul insists that this is not the case. It's impossible to imagine anyone more ethnically Jewish than Paul – he even lists his credentials – and he is part of God's messianic people. God has not rejected that category Paul refers to as 'foreknown'. This rejection of some along with the retention of the foreknown has happened at other times. Paul mentions the time of Elijah. Those retained, by grace, are called 'a remnant'. Israel, as a whole, went astray but Israel, as a remnant, received grace. As is often the case, Paul makes his point on the basis of Isaiah and the Psalms. Nevertheless, Paul is not without hope for the part of Israel that is not within the remnant. The setback may only be temporary. God has a purpose in mind. Israel will become jealous of the Gentiles who are receiving God's blessing. The stumbling of Israel has given an opportunity for Gentiles to become a part of the people of God and so has brought blessing to the whole world. If that's what Israel can do by stumbling, just imagine what it might achieve through being restored!

2 The cultivated olive tree as an image of the people of God

Romans 11:13–24

Paul turns his attention to his non-Jewish hearers. He's proud of his ministry to Gentiles like them. One of the possible results of that ministry is that it might provoke jealousy among some of ethnic Israel and lead them to become part of the people of the Messiah. This could be like resurrection! Israel, explains Paul, is like a tree with holy roots which lead to holy branches. However, some of those branches – that is, some of the Jewish people – have, because they have not believed what God has done through Messiah Jesus, been cut off and non-Jews – that is, the Gentile Christians – have been grafted into the tree in their place and so benefit from the roots. This should generate deep gratitude among the Gentile Christians and give them absolutely no sense of superiority over the lost branches. Be sure to stay faithful, says Paul to the Gentiles in his audience, or you too might be lost. At one and the same time, it all illustrates both the generosity and the severity of God. And those parts of ethnic Israel that have been lost might yet be recovered if they come to have faith in what God is doing. Bringing them back into the fold would be a lot more straightforward than bringing in non-Jews because Jewish people are naturally a part of God's cultivated olive tree, and the Gentiles are not.

3. God's pattern in his dealings with humanity provokes wonder and praise

Romans 11:25–36

Paul summarises his argument. What we have learned is that those God has foreknown, whether belonging to ethnic Israel or not, now form the people of God. This group is identified by its allegiance to Messiah Jesus. Part of ethnic Israel is experiencing unbelief, and this is creating space for people from other ethnic groups to become a part of God's family. Israel is thus defined in terms of the Messiah.

Before Jesus came, spiritual Israel was the part of ethnic Israel that trusted that God would keep his promises and this group is now joined by those, both Jew and Gentile, who recognise that God has acted through Messiah Jesus, to keep those promises. This is the people of God and therefore the group of humanity that will experience God's salvation. To put it another way, this is the process by which all Israel – all the people of God through Messiah Jesus – will be saved. Paul then makes his case from the scriptures. The Messiah is the deliverer who has taken away the sins of his people by renewing his covenant promises. Paul understands the text as a reference to the continuing mission of the church to Jews and Gentiles. All those foreknown by God will be a part of God's people.

Paul has found a pattern through which the unbelieving part of ethnic Israel has helped lead to the inclusion of once disobedient non-Jews within God's people. Paul dares hope that the now disobedient part of ethnic Israel might, in their turn, come to faith, receive mercy and be (re)integrated into the people of God. In this astonishing plan, every category of humanity has been disobedient and has received God's mercy. Small wonder that the apostle concludes with a hymn of praise to the unsearchable purposes of God.

4. Our response to the gospel – worship and transformation

In the light of all this – that is, the conclusions of chapters 8 and 11 – Paul makes his appeal using language that is drawn from the temple. He takes the language of sacrifice and uses it as a metaphor – one which goes to the heart of what literal sacrifices were intended to demonstrate. God's people no longer respond to God by offering the lives of animals. We respond by wholeheartedly offering our own lives in God's service. This is the heart of true worship. Paul calls for the worship of God as a way of life and as a process of inner transformation. He will go on to spell out what he hopes to see.

First of all, Paul appeals for some self-awareness. All the believers should make a realistic appraisal of themselves and their contribution. They belong to Jesus, and they belong to the church. They should understand themselves in the light of this, and not imagine they are more significant than they are. Then he goes on to remind all the Christians in Rome that they are a part of one body. Each is a member of that body and so each belongs to all the others. They are organically related to one another, and each part is impacted by things that happen to the other parts. All have different gifts and so all have a part to play. Paul outlines a number of different ways that people can serve but he has no intention of being exhaustive. The church has room for contributions of all kinds. Interestingly, there appears to be no hierarchy of gifting. It's true that prophecy comes first but leading comes near the end of the list. It seems that every contribution is equally significant and equally valued.

5. Following Jesus

In these verses, Paul continues to spell out what it means to follow Jesus. The focus is on love and its practical expressions. A useful prayer exercise might be to consider our own lives against the qualities and practices the apostle outlines here. The key issue is genuine love. This is love that is not self-serving but is focused on others. It's one of the great issues in literature, from the tragedy of *King Lear* to those characters in old novels whose attention to older relatives is driven by expectations of a legacy rather than true concern for their well-being. To what extent can we claim that we find ourselves in these words? It might be easier to know the answer in some cases – giving to the people of God, offering hospitality to strangers – than it is in others. How can we measure zeal or ardour? Nevertheless, these are good questions to ask ourselves. Not to give us a sense of failure but to encourage us to continue to seek the renewal that Paul speaks of earlier in the chapter.

6. Forgiveness and overcoming evil

Romans 12:14–21

Occasionally, you may read about scholars who are trying to make a name for themselves by arguing that Paul somehow betrayed Jesus or cared nothing for his teachings. Yet the exhortations here seem to owe everything to Jesus. The words appear to be a kind of summary of the ideas we read in the gospels. Consider reading through the passage slowly and then through the sermon on the mount in Matthew 5—7, and see how the teachings compare.

One of Paul's concerns is that Christians should be forgiving people. People have written whole books about the subject but at the very heart of the idea is that if we are wronged, we should not try to get our own back. Paul says we should leave these things to 'the wrath' (v. 19) – the words 'of God' are not in the Greek. Wrath is the thing that motivates those responsible for justice. This may be a human authority as at 13:4–5 or God as at 1:18 or 2:5. Instead of seeking revenge, we should treat those who make themselves our enemies as we would our friends and family. Paul insists, quoting from Proverbs, that this will seem like a form of judgement! The key principle is stated at the end of the chapter and this rests on Paul's conviction that however things may appear, in the end, good will triumph over evil. To do good is to take the winning side in a spiritual battle.

Guidelines

The issues addressed in chapters 9—11 concern Israel, God's ancient covenant people. These matters have kept cropping up during Paul's argument and he has given holding answers up to this point. Now, he addresses the questions in full. His answer takes him on a journey from deep anguish at the start of chapter 9 to praise and wonder at the end of chapter 11. In reflecting on the scriptures and on God's purposes, Paul has come to a place where he can see how his own sadness and deep questioning find their place within an astonishing vision of God's dealings with the whole of humanity, Jews and non-Jews, Israel and the Gentiles.

From here, Paul can begin his exploration of the implications of this teaching for the believers in Rome. He sets out what it means for them to follow Jesus in their context. As he does so, his words echo down the centuries speaking to the people of God in every generation, including our own.

- One of the great questions in Jewish-Christian dialogue concerns the relationship between the church and Israel. The picture of the olive tree is one of the ways Paul can be understood to contribute to the discussion. In what ways is the image helpful or unhelpful in inter-faith discussions today?

- Paul's reflections lead him to see a pattern of disobedience and mercy in God's dealings with both Israel and the nations (11:30–32). He sees this as grounds to end his reflection in wonder at the overarching purposes of God. Is this a helpful way to end the argument? Should all our discussions of God and God's purposes end in an acknowledgement of mystery and in doxology (11:33–36)?

- At the start of chapter 12, Paul summarises the appropriate response to all that he has explained up to this point. Drawing on the language of the temple, Paul asks for a living sacrifice that involves an inner transformation that leads to an understanding of – and presumably obedience to – the will of God. Can you see how one leads to the other? And is this a helpful way to summarise the life of discipleship?

- One of Paul's favourite themes is unity. Here, and elsewhere, he expresses this through the image of the church as a body. One aspect of recognising that we are part of a body is acknowledging our need for others, seeing our own contribution as just one among many, and therefore having an appropriate estimate of ourselves. Can you think of anywhere where this message needs to be heard?

- Think about the parallels between Paul's words in the second half of chapter 12 with the teachings of Jesus in the gospels. How true is Paul's teaching to that of the Lord himself?
- To what extent do we live up to the virtues and practices Paul teaches in chapter 12:9–21?
- Paul talks about the need to avoid vengeance (12:19). Some see this as a full understanding of forgiveness, but others believe there is more to it than that. What approach would you take?

FURTHER READING

Matthew W. Bates, *Salvation by Allegiance Alone: Rethinking Faith, works and the gospel of Jesus the king* (Baker, 2017).

Michael F. Bird, *The Saving Righteousness of God: Studies on Paul, justification and the new perspective* (Paternoster, 2007).

Karl P. Donfried, ed., *The Romans Debate*, revised and expanded edition (T & T Clark, 1991).

Paula Gooder, *Phoebe: A story* (Hodder, 2018).

Richard N. Longenecker, *Introducing Romans: Critical issues in Paul's most famous letter* (Eerdmans, 2011).

Richard N. Longenecker, *The Epistle to the Romans* (Eerdmans, 2016).

Peter Oakes, *Reading Romans in Pompeii: Paul's letter at ground level* (SPCK, 2009).

Thomas R. Schreiner, *Romans*, second edition (Baker, 2018).

John Stott, *The Message of Romans: God's good news for the world* (IVP, 1994).

Anthony C. Thiselton, *Discovering Romans: Content, interpretation, reception* (Eerdmans, 2016).

A.J.M. Wedderburn, *The Reasons for Romans* (T&T Clark, 1991).

Tom Wright, *Justification: God's plan and Paul's vision,* (SPCK, 2009).

Ruth

Steve Walton

Much of life is a 'messy middle', when events or people seem against us: bereavement, job loss, house move, kids' difficulties at school or retirement. The book of Ruth involves migration, refugees, bereavement and bitterness, and shows how God works with his people through these tough times.

It is set in troubled times in Israel: the period of the judges (1:1), between 1400 and 1100BC. These are lawless days, when everyone does what is right in their own eyes (Judges 17:6; 21:25). Think: Wild West in cowboy movies. Ruth opens a window into ordinary Israelites' lives: the characters are not the great and powerful, but farmers, widows, refugees. There are three key human characters: Naomi, Ruth and Boaz.

Naomi is a double refugee, having migrated with her husband Elimelech to Moab during a famine (1:1–2), and then returning to Bethlehem as a bereaved widow and mother (1:3–6). Naomi maintains her faith in the God of Israel in Moab, as Ruth the Moabite recognises (1:16–17), and yet returns home as a broken woman. At one level, the book tells the story of her recovery.

Ruth is from Moab, the widow of Mahlon, Naomi's son (4:10). She loves Naomi deeply and is determined to go with her (1:18). She commits herself to Israel's God in doing so (1:16). She acts with courage and resourcefulness, taking initiative (2:2) and adopting Naomi's plan (3:1–9).

Boaz is a man of standing (2:1), a farmer and businessman. He is a relation of Naomi's late husband and has a particular responsibility for Elimelech's family. He is generous and kind towards Ruth and Naomi, and is a wise negotiator in their interests.

God is only mentioned twice as acting (1:6; 4:13). Nevertheless, the way events turn out shows God's hand at work and, ultimately, he will bring amazing fruit from this ancient love story.

Unless otherwise stated, Bible quotations are from the NIV. These notes will also work well with the NRSV.

1 A tragic tale

Ruth 1:1–7

Think of how movies or TV dramas tell stories: sometimes long periods of time fly by in a few on-screen seconds, and at other times the storytelling slows down to show viewers the moment-by-moment development of crucial events. We enter the book of Ruth in one of those 'time flies by' sections: these verses cover more than ten years (v. 4). The author is setting the scene for the story of this short book with key information.

First, we meet the Israelites Elimelech and his wife Naomi, from Bethlehem (ironically meaning 'house of bread') in Judah but emigrating because of famine to the other side of the Dead Sea to Moab, accompanied by their sons Mahlon and Kilion (vv. 1–2). They aren't the first biblical characters to migrate in famine: Abraham and Isaac do it too (Genesis 12:10; 26:1), and such travel was common in the ancient world. However, Moab is a traditional enemy of Israel; they worship the god Chemosh (1 Kings 11:33), and so this is a place of spiritual danger for worshippers of Israel's God. As refugees, they are hoping for better than the place they left, and yet are aware that they are different from the people of their new place and thus potentially subject to prejudice and harm.

Tragedy follows, for Naomi experiences triple bereavement in the death of her husband (v. 3) and then the death of her two (now-married) sons (v. 5). So Naomi is left as the head of a household of two other widows, her Moabite daughters-in-law Ruth and Orpah (v. 4). Naomi lacks financial security, for she has no husband to provide for her. The usual options open to her are slavery or prostitution. Her situation is bleak – she will describe it later as the Lord turning his hand against her (1:13) and dealing harshly with her (1:21).

Nevertheless, Naomi engages with the situation, rather than giving up. When good news comes that the Lord has ended the famine (v. 6 – the first mention of God in the book), she decides to return to Bethlehem (v. 7). Surely there will be something better in her homeland and hometown, especially since God has blessed Israel by a fresh harvest. Naturally, Ruth and Orpah accompany Naomi and, as we picture the opening titles rolling on the movie, we wonder what will happen to these three widows.

2 Turning a corner

Ruth 1:8–21

After the rapid overview of the first seven verses, the book slows down and this section takes place over a few days, inviting us to pay careful attention to the conversation between Naomi and her daughters-in-law.

Naomi has evidently kept her faith in Israel's God while in Moab, for she speaks about the Lord, the covenant name of God (vv. 8, 9, 13, 21) and wants him to do good for Orpah and Ruth (vv. 8–9). She has nothing to offer them and believes God is against her (vv. 11–13, 20–21). Upon Naomi's return home to Bethlehem, the local women even question, 'Can this be Naomi?' (v. 19), implying she is physically changed by her grim experiences. Naomi means 'pleasant' or 'lovely', but she wants to be called 'Mara', 'bitter' (v. 20). For these reasons, Naomi gives Orpah and Ruth a way out, inviting them to return to Moab, where they may find husbands (vv. 8–9).

Orpah accepts Naomi's offer, and we hear no more of her (v. 14). But Ruth, remarkably, 'clung' to Naomi (v. 14) – the same word used of a man clinging to his wife (Genesis 2:24, NRSV), signalling deep commitment. Notice how much Ruth uses 'you' and 'your' (vv. 16–17): she really wants to stay with Naomi. Her commitment is not only to Naomi, but also to Naomi's God: 'your God my God' and then she names the Lord (v. 17). Ruth has evidently seen something in Naomi which draws her to Israel's God, and she's wholehearted about this decision: she will even go to the point of death (v. 17). Ruth stakes her life on the Lord, rather than going back to the land of the god Chemosh, even though she can have no idea what this will bring.

Where is God in this story? Naomi is in the 'messy middle' of bereavement, being a refugee and feeling hurt by God. And yet she twice calls the Lord 'the Almighty' (vv. 20, 21). She understands that God reigns and complains about how God is treating her (vv. 13, 21). Amid this, she (indirectly) asks God's blessing on Orpah and Ruth (vv. 8–9), showing her hope for God's blessing in the future, even if faint. Naomi speaks *about* God in this passage, but there is no indication that she speaks *to* God as the psalms of personal lament do (e.g. Psalms 6, 130). Nevertheless, God hears Naomi, he hasn't forgotten or abandoned her and he is planning good things for her through Ruth.

3 Back in Bethlehem with Boaz

Here, the third key human character is introduced: Boaz. He has land and hires reapers to gather his crops. He's related to Naomi's husband (v. 1). Ruth doesn't know this until later (vv. 19–22), but the author lets us in on this information now. Naomi does not approach Boaz before he meets Ruth, perhaps because she is ashamed.

Gleaning is a key activity here, mentioned multiple times (vv. 2–3, 7, 8, 15–19, 23), always with Ruth as the gleaner. Israelite law provides for people in poverty – widows, orphans and resident foreigners– by allowing them to gather harvest leftovers: stray stalks of grain, plus any sheaves the reapers left behind (Deuteronomy 24:19). Reapers should not harvest to the edges of the field but should leave grain in the margins for needy people (Leviticus 19:9; 23:22). Ruth certainly qualifies, for she is both a widow and a resident foreigner.

The potential problems in gleaning are real, though. Male reapers might sexually harass a woman gleaning, particularly if she was young. They could make it harder for gleaners to gather much. Ruth struck gold in her chosen field, for not only was Boaz's foreman helpful in giving her permission to glean (vv. 6–7), but when Boaz appears he is generous beyond the law's require-ments. 'As it turned out' (v. 3) signals God's providence in taking Ruth there. Boaz is impressed by Ruth's care for Naomi (v. 11) and recognises Ruth's commitment to Israel's God (v. 12). So he advises her to stay in his field with other young women gleaning and he ensures that his reapers will not harass her (vv. 8–9). Moreover, he tells his reapers to help her by pulling grain stalks from the sheaves to glean (vv. 15–16).

Ruth gleans a large amount (v. 17): an ephah is 12–13 kilos, worth about two weeks' wages at the time. When Ruth returns home and Naomi learns that Boaz has been generous and kind, Naomi's dark mood changes: she thanks God for Boaz and for God's kindness through Boaz (v. 20). 'Kindness' is a rich word for God's loyal love and for such love among his people: we saw it twice in 1:8. Further, Boaz is a 'guardian-redeemer' (NIV), 'one with the right to redeem' (NRSV note) – in law, he has responsibility for his late relative's family, to keep his property in the family (Leviticus 25:25–55). God's hand is on these two women, and Naomi is starting to see that.

4 A surprising proposal

Ruth 3:1–18

The barley and wheat harvests take two months (2:23). Perhaps Naomi hopes Boaz will propose marriage to Ruth. In that society, the parents arrange marriage, normally by the respective fathers negotiating. That possibility is not open to Naomi, so she devises a daring and risky plan to persuade Boaz to marry Ruth.

Ruth is to wash, perfume herself and wear her best clothes (v. 3) – all marks of a woman prepared for her wedding (Ezekiel 16:8–12). Then she is to go to Boaz at the public threshing floor at night. But that is a men's place, especially at night: the only women there then would be prostitutes (see Hosea 9:1). Ruth may be seen by other men and attacked, particularly if they were drunk after harvest celebrations. And the outcome is entirely in Boaz's hands – he might take advantage of Ruth to have sex. Ruth raises the stakes even on this high-risk strategy.

Boaz sleeps behind the grain heap, giving some privacy (v. 7). Ruth's uncovering Boaz's feet causes him to 'shudder' from the cold (a better translation than 'startled', v. 8) and wake to the shock of finding a woman there. It's dark, and his initial assumption may be that this is a prostitute seeking custom – hence his question, 'Who are you?' (v. 9). Rather than follow Naomi's plan and wait for Boaz to tell her what to do (v. 4), Ruth asks Boaz to spread the corner of his garment over her, literally 'to spread the *wing*', using the same word as 2:12. It's a Hebrew idiom for marriage (Ezekiel 16:8) – remarkably, Ruth proposes marriage to Boaz, a daring request for a woman significantly younger than Boaz and a foreigner, and especially so in these circumstances. More, she urges him to act because he is a guardian-redeemer (v. 9, NIV) with legal responsibility to care for Elimelech's family.

Boaz is willing, although he's surprised to have this proposal, recognising that Ruth could have sought a younger husband (v. 10). However, another guardian-redeemer is a closer relative, so he has prior responsibility for Ruth and Naomi (v. 12). Boaz honourably commits himself to act on this and to act quickly (v. 13). Throughout, he invokes the Lord's name in thanksgiving (v. 10) and as his witness (v. 13) – this is a godly man. Indeed, Boaz sends Ruth away with a gift of barley, perhaps the first instalment of a wedding gift to Naomi (vv. 15, 17).

5 Marriage and land in the town gate

Ruth 4:1–12

Here, the focus shifts from the female focus so far, with Naomi and Ruth at its heart, to a male-dominated scene. The patriarchal society is clear, and God works in ways which engage with the realities of that society. This part of the story tackles the question of whom Ruth will marry.

This is a vivid scene, set in the town gate where men gather to do business. It is probably a substantial building with rooms in the sides of the gateway itself. God's timing is evident in the other guardian-redeemer appearing just as Boaz arrives (v. 1; compare God's hand in Ruth's choice of field, 2:3). The translation 'friend' for the other guardian-redeemer renders an odd phrase which means 'Mr So-and-so': the author conceals his name, for it is irrelevant. Boaz assembles ten of the town elders, whose presence makes this a formal, legal setting (vv. 2, 4).

Boaz then gives new information to the story: literally, 'Let me uncover your ear' (v. 4). There is land involved: maybe Elimelech sold it and the guardian-redeemer could repurchase it for the family; perhaps it was left while Naomi was in Moab and now needs selling to support her and Ruth. This sounds like a good deal, and Mr So-and-so jumps at it! But then, Boaz introduces the complication that with the land goes Ruth's hand in marriage (v. 5). Israelite law requires a brother to marry his dead brother's widow if there are no children, and to have children on behalf of his brother (Deuteronomy 25:5–10). But we know no requirement in Israelite law connecting redeeming land with marrying a relative's childless widow. It may have been a custom at this time, or perhaps Boaz is putting public moral pressure on Mr So-and-so. Mr So-and-so withdraws as a result – he cannot do both things (v. 6).

We then learn the custom of handing over a sandal to formalise a business deal (v. 7): the author's explanation shows that the book is written significantly later. Boaz thus gains the right to buy the field and to marry Ruth and makes a formal declaration in the presence of the ten elder-witnesses that he will do so (vv. 9–10).

Interestingly, Boaz mentions Ruth's Moabite nationality twice in this section (vv. 5, 10), making it clear that she is being incorporated into Israel – having taken refuge under the Lord's wings, she is now also under Boaz's protection (see notes in section 4 on 2:12; 3:9).

6 To us a child is born!

For only the second time in the book, God is said to act directly, here in giving Ruth and Boaz a child (v. 13); the previous occasion was restoring food and harvest to the land (1:6). Ruth was childless for perhaps ten years (1:4–5) and belongs among other childless women in scripture to whom God gives a child (e.g. Genesis 17:19, 21; 18:9–10; 21:1–3; 25:21; 29:31–32; 30:22–24). Ruth is a 'woman of *noble character*' (3:11), using the same word as for Boaz, the 'man of *standing*' (2:1) – and God loves and blesses their marriage with a child.

The focus here, though, is on Naomi, who is a transformed woman. She was bitter (1:20), but now is happy, cuddling her grandson (v. 16). She was empty (1:21), but now is full, for she has three people in her life (Ruth, Boaz and Obed), mirroring the three she lost (Elimelech, Mahlon and Chilion). Naomi passes from triple bereavement (1:3–5) to restored life (v. 15). This has all come through Ruth, and the author hints that *Ruth* is also Naomi's guardian-redeemer (v. 14), without excluding Boaz. Indeed, one Ruth is better than seven sons – the number of perfection (v. 15), and the women of the town embrace Naomi and Ruth into their circle (v. 17).

Just when we thought this was simply a lovely ancient love story, the author shows us that God is working here with his big purposes of history in mind (v. 17). Ruth the Moabite is great King David's great-grandmother; the greatest king of Israel is not a pure-bred Israelite at all! The mini-genealogy which closes the book (vv. 18–22) presents edited highlights of Perez's family, down to David (see the fuller genealogy in 1 Chronicles 2). We met Perez in the blessing of Boaz and Ruth (4:12); Perez's birth resulted from Judah having sex with Tamar, his daughter-in-law, after her husband Er's death (Genesis 38). And Er himself was the result of Judah marrying a Canaanite woman, Shua. Israel's history is full of messy family life!

God plays a long game in working in history. Matthew gives Ruth an honoured place in his genealogy of Jesus (Matthew 1:5), one of four non-Israelite women included, alongside Tamar (Matthew 1:3), Rahab (Matthew 1:5) and Bathsheba, Uriah's wife (Matthew 1:6). So Jesus himself is not from pure-bred Israelite stock, either – God's love for the world extends to including the world in his family.

Guidelines

The book of Ruth sees events through women's eyes, by contrast with the stories of men in much of scripture. Ruth and Naomi are women of their time, and they work with the social and cultural constraints of their time and place. They're concerned for security, which means a husband and children (3:1; 4:11). They understand possible dangers to women: Ruth could be molested by the reapers (2:9, 22) and her reputation might be damaged by spending the night with Boaz (3:13–14). These women know how the world of men works: Naomi recognises they need to wait to see how things play out when Boaz talks with the other male guardian-redeemer (3:18).

This book makes women and their concerns visible. It shows us the situation of ancient Israel, which is very different to the west today. It's not saying, of course, that Christian women today should be like Naomi and Ruth, leaving men to run things. But it is offering female models of discipleship from which believers, both women *and* men, can learn (as is true also for the male models of discipleship in scripture). Ruth and Naomi invite us to reflect on how we respond to dire circumstances with trust in God, imagination, creativity and boldness. They encourage us that God stands with his people in tough times and walks with them through to the other side of those times. God doesn't take the problems away, but he does provide ways through them.

The book is certainly not anti-men, for the key male character, Boaz, is an honourable and godly man who acts for Ruth and Naomi's welfare. In this, Boaz offers us a model of how people with power can act in godly and just ways to support those who lack power.

FURTHER READING

Havilah Dharamraj with Philip Ewan Yalla, *Ruth: A pastoral and contextual commentary* (Langham Global Library, 2019) – an insightful study by an Indian Bible teacher and scholar, drawing on her south Asian context in reading Ruth.

Richard Bauckham, *Is the Bible Male? The book of Ruth and biblical narrative* (Grove, 1996) – a fine short study which highlights the female-centred storytelling in Ruth.

David Atkinson, The Message of Ruth: Wings of refuge, revised edition (IVP, 2022) – a section-by-section study drawing out key themes and ideas.

Deuteronomy: ethics for the people of God

Ashley Hibbard

I get strange looks when I tell people that my favourite book of the Bible is Deuteronomy. It's not a top pick for very many people. What could possibly be so compelling about law? And didn't Jesus do away with it?

There are many laws in Deuteronomy that are immediately applicable to real issues in our day. Of course, the precise form of the law is no longer binding; we are citizens of a new covenant. But while the form of the law may no longer apply, the function of the law is timeless. The purpose of the law reveals the values of God himself. While some passages are difficult and require a lot of work to extract the principle and a modern application, many are quite obvious, quite challenging and quite prone to step on our toes. It doesn't take much examination of the statutes to come up with modern issues to which Deuteronomy speaks: Generous giving. Care for the poor. Giving God the best. Sufficiently supporting ministers. Creation care. Neighbour care. Adultery. Rape. Human trafficking. Honest business transactions.

In some ways, it's actually odd that Deuteronomy has been so neglected. I hope its neglect is only a result of it seeming unapproachable. I hope that it is not because of the deep and all-encompassing demands that scripture places on our lives. Without a doubt, we are a people of grace. But let us not forget that the law was a form of grace, a gift from a loving God to his often-wayward people. But with great grace comes great responsibility, to live according to the ethics not of our world, or our denomination, or our political party, but according to the ethics of our good and great king.

So come and give Deuteronomy a fair shake in these next two weeks. By the time we're done, it might not be your favourite book, but maybe you'll understand why it's mine.

Unless otherwise stated, Bible quotations are taken from the ESV.

1 The party tithe

It is a measure of God's intent to bless Israel materially that he required subsistence farmers to provide not one but two tithes. One tithe we speak of often: the tithe to support the widows, orphans, and Levites. A discussion of that tithe, and how (or whether) it is a part of the new covenant, is outside the scope of this reflection, but we will explore the second tithe now.

There's something that seems wasteful in dedicating a tithe to a party, and even with the relatively high percentage of optional income in the developed world, it would be very hard to imagine spending £3,000 on a yearly party!

But there are two things that make this party more understandable than it might first appear. First, it is not celebration for its own sake, but rather to learn to fear the Lord and to celebrate before him. At first, these might sound to our ears like opposite goals. But there's something beautiful about learning fear – or perhaps 'reverence' would be a better way of thinking of it here – through a party. It reminds the people that their ultimate provider is their God, not their land. If their God has told them to spend their produce in a way that may seem frivolous, then he can be trusted to supply their needs. And that kind of God, that kind of generous provider, is worth celebrating.

Second, this is not a private party. This is a party to which others should be invited. In particular view in this text are Levites (v. 29). As the Levites had virtually no land and their income was almost entirely based on the other tithe, they had no means by which to celebrate the goodness and abundant provision of God. How would they learn both the fear and the celebration of the Lord? By being invited to the party of others.

While there is much that is good about careful stewardship (economic modesty is a New Testament virtue – 1 Timothy 6:8–10), perhaps we have elevated these virtues to a level where celebration, even holy and generous celebrations, might be frowned upon. We need to be careful of our tendencies to asceticism, which only has 'an appearance of wisdom… but… no value in stopping the indulgence of the flesh' (Colossians 2:23).

2 The limits of indebtedness

Deuteronomy 15:1–11

Socialists frequently read biblical law as promoting socialism. Capitalists frequently read biblical law as promoting capitalism. But there is no name for the economic system described in Deuteronomy. While certain aspects of the law happen to align with certain systems, there is no human economic system that would allow for mass defaulting on every loan every seven years. The economy described by God seems unworkable; the divine balance sheet cannot be reconciled with human maths. God's unworkable system taught his people to give with no expectation of repayment. There's even a verse for people (like me, honestly) who might try to take measures against losing money: an admonition not to withhold loans when the Sabbath year is near. Such an inclination is even described as an issue, not of logic, but of the heart, with such people described as 'unworthy' (v. 9) and 'grudging' (v. 10).

But God continues to call his people to a radical, perhaps even irresponsible, generosity. As we saw with the party tithe, this is a matter of reliance on his provision. He is the ultimate owner of the land that his people work, of the crops they produce and the flocks they tend. He is convinced that no act of generosity is beyond his ability to resupply. He expects his people to be comfortable with these unsolvable accounting problems.

Very often, Jesus' words in the sermon on the mount are perceived to be radical words of the new covenant. And while some of what he says is new, most is very old. The sort of generosity taught by Jesus, the sort that goes beyond what is asked for to give what is needed, does not start with his teaching, but with the teachings here in Deuteronomy. God required his people to have strict limits to human indebtedness, the flip side of which is unlimited generosity. We have no reason to believe that Israel ever functioned this way, and no one has ever figured out how it might have worked practically. But perhaps that's the lesson: that God's economy is not limited by human practicality.

3 Celebrating before the Lord

Deuteronomy 16:1–17

The English word 'holiday' is a compound of the words 'holy day', and that's an apt term, not in the sense of 'godly' but in the sense of 'set apart'. They represent more than just an extra eight hours not working. Holidays involve traditions and rituals and expectations. Typically, they're not so much about relaxation as about cultivating family and community.

We have already seen in Deuteronomy that God has provided time off for his people, through the rhythms of sabbath days and sabbath years. But here he provides them with holidays: time to celebrate God's past goodness and deliverance, and to spend time as families and communities. God wanted his people to have regular rhythms and rituals that would help them to internalise his goodness. The best learning is often experiential, and thus these festivals were meant to be active reminders and educational experiences that would help Israel to appreciate the God who worked mightily in history for their good and who worked through ordinary, yet still mighty, means to provide for them year by year. And as they learned and remembered these truths themselves, they were well positioned to include their families and their children, and to use these days and these rituals to pass their faith on to the next generation.

Three holidays are described briefly in this chapter, but we will consider only Passover here. Passover coincided with the beginning of the barley harvest. It is interesting that in Deuteronomy 16:3, Moses tells Israel that they will eat 'the bread of affliction,' as the ESV puts it, but it could just be translated 'humble bread'. And the bread would likely have been humble not only because it wasn't leavened, but also because barley bread was considered inferior to wheat bread. The bread at Passover was the simplest, most basic, most humble bread. And that brings us to the far more important aspect of Passover: the deliverance from Egypt. That the bread was unleavened would have reminded them of the haste with which they left Egypt, and the humility of the bread would have reminded them of what was likely the very humble food that they subsisted on as slaves. Passover is first and foremost about the deliverance of the powerless, the story of a king who will stop at nothing to free his enslaved people and fulfil his promises. Eating humble bread at a festival like Passover would help them to see how far they had come.

4 Impartial justice

Deuteronomy 16:18–20; 19:15–21

In Deuteronomy 16:18, God commands that judges should be appointed from within the tribes to judge their own people. This is the first of a couple of places in this passage that emphasise the importance of leadership arising from within a community. That God then speaks directly to those judges is a less common feature in biblical law, and probably indicates some degree of emphasis. The significance of his requirement that they be fair and not to accept bribes is easily missed, but cannot be overstated. Bribery in the ancient world was incredibly common. Laws against bribery were few and appear to have been inconsistently applied. This command to seek only justice, and not personal gain, was completely countercultural. The person who wins should not be the person with the most buying power. Truth should not be bought.

Deuteronomy 19:15–21 is concerned about witnesses, and again the main point is that the truth of a matter is crucial. The problem with a case where there is only one witness – the person with the complaint – and defendant is that the louder or more charismatic person tends to be considered right. And so God requires two 'witnesses'. At times, this passage has been misconstrued to mean that a wrong can't be reported if someone else did not see it. This is a gross misreading of the text. The term translated 'witness' in Hebrew can encompass what we think of as both 'witness' and 'evidence'. For example, Exodus 22:13 talks about what a shepherd should do if an animal in his care is attacked by wild animals, and it says, 'If it is torn by beasts, let him bring it as evidence.' That word 'evidence' is the same as the word 'witness'. The shepherd in that case has two witnesses; his own word and the physical evidence of the remains of the animal. Let us be careful to listen to those whose accusations have indeed come by two witnesses: their own and their evidence.

Notice that 'witnesses' are verifiable. An oath doesn't count as a witness. You cannot use divination to discern which person is telling the truth. You cannot perform an ordeal. (In fact, trial by ordeal is almost completely absent from biblical law.) Justice is a matter of observable fact, not a matter of faith, or charisma, or status. It's only a matter of truth. Without truth, there can be no justice.

5 Kingship

Put in modern terms, God says in verses 15–17, 'If you have a king, he must limit his military technology, limit his economic power, limit his political alliances and limit his wealth.' Horses and chariots were the best in military technology at that time; any king who wanted to stay current and dominate the battlefield had to have a well-stocked stable of horses. But here, God calls Israel's kings to limit their trade relations with Egypt, especially with regard to horses. Egypt was usually one of the wealthier nations of the ancient world, and certainly the most politically stable. They would have been a great trading partner. But God called them out of Egypt; he doesn't want Israel getting too cosy with their place of suffering and slavery. The king was also not to have many wives. Marrying wives was how you made political alliances in the ancient world, providing security and often gifts.

Not only was the king required to limit most of the things that made him look kingly, but God also said that he had to write out his own copy of the law and study it daily. That doesn't sound much like a king either. Kings should be making alliances, giving directives, collecting taxes, looking impressive, enjoying good food – not poring over a manuscript and making a painstakingly exact copy of it, and then studying it constantly. That's what priests do! And I think that's the point. God did not want his people led by a worldly king. He had to be God's kind of king, with God's priorities of justice and faithfulness and righteousness.

Leadership matters, and yet leadership structures are often desperately fallen and broken. Recurring scandals in politics have made that abundantly clear, but it has always been true. God tried to put guardrails in place, to allow for the leadership that his people needed, while attempting to avoid the worst of the corruption and excesses that tend to accompany it.

6 Environmental responsibility

Deuteronomy 20:19–20; 22:6–7

It is surprising that there is so much resistance in some Christian circles to the matter of environmental concern. Creation care is not an optional extra for the people of God. In Genesis 2:15 we are told that God placed Adam in the garden to work and keep it, and most people would see a general principle there that God calls all of humanity to care for the world for which we have been appointed stewards. Certainly, environmentalism can be taken too far. Giving personhood to rivers is not likely to be what God had in mind when he instructed Adam to work and to keep creation. But overemphasising a matter does not negate the importance of correct emphasis. Several biblical laws provide specific guidance on how to live out the principle of creation care. While creation is ours to use, it is not ours to use thoughtlessly. Sustainability matters.

Despite its position as the concluding statute in a section concerned with just war, this law in Deuteronomy 20:19–20 demonstrates surprising ecological nuance. God tells his people that when they have besieged a city, they must not build their siege works with the wood of fruit trees. They must be certain only to use trees that don't provide food. God is not in favour of scorched earth tactics. Win or lose, someone will live in that city and need food to eat. However important this battle is (or is perceived to be), it cannot be carried out in such a way that people's future and safety is affected.

The law about chicks and eggs in Deuteronomy 22:6–7 has a similar concern for sustainability. The reasoning is likely that the mother bird can have more young, but without the mother, not only will there never be more young from her, the eggs and young that she does have won't survive. To use a modern term, I think what God is requiring here is an effort on our part to have a light ecological footprint.

The image of stewardship provides us a middle way between uncaring abuse of creation and elevating creation to a status that it was never meant to have. Creation is not ours, but it has been entrusted to us. We are the holders and caretakers of that trust. Our use of it is right, but only when that use is thoughtful and careful, respecting both the one who entrusted it to us and those who will take up the trust after us.

Guidelines

Many of the laws in this week's readings are deeply concerned with both personal and corporate responsibility. The responsibility to tithe, to enact impartial justice, to lead with holiness and humility, to care for creation – these are all matters of great importance in scripture. I think it is incredibly significant that issues that the modern world tends to divide into categories of 'moral' and 'justice' don't seem to be divided similarly in scripture. Issues of justice, of morality and of worship all jumble together. For a certain sector of our churches to be concerned about issues popularly considered 'justice', but not morality is a great misuse of scripture. And for a certain sector of our churches to be concerned about issues popularly considered 'morality', but not justice is an equal misuse of scripture.

The reason for this (apparent) jumbling of laws in Deuteronomy is that they are all matters of worship. Right worship is not only a matter of our devotional acts and corporate gatherings, but pervades every aspect of our lives. As we allow God's light to shine in the dark and dusty corners that we neglect in our hearts, we find ourselves called to consider with what sins we find ourselves too comfortable, and to commit ourselves once more to an obedient discipleship. We are not to be conformed to the age in which we find ourselves, but transformed through the renewal of our minds; this will allow us to see more clearly what God's own priorities are, and to shape our lives to match them (Romans 12:2–3). Therefore let us cooperate with the Holy Spirit in this process of transformation into the likeness of Christ, to be a people who are equal to the challenges before us, both in the church that our Lord died for and in the world that he loves.

1 The God who condones war rape?

Deuteronomy 21:10–14

This may be scripture's most ethically problematic law. Whether or not the woman is subjected to physical violence, she is powerless to refuse this man's sexual use of her, and such a gross power imbalance and lack of ability to consent absolutely constitutes rape. This is horrifying, and I would suggest that God is just as horrified as we are – and he is the one who spoke it.

The principle of divine accommodation suggests that throughout scripture, God makes allowances for human finitude and sinfulness. We see the righteous God sometimes choose to regulate his people's unrighteousness, rather than trying to prevent it. For example, God allows slavery, but regulates it by prohibiting debilitating beatings, mutilation and human trafficking.

The horror of this text pales by comparison to what God was trying to prevent. In the ancient Near East, war rape was not just common, it was expected. When cities were captured, attacking soldiers were free to rape any women they found. It was not only a matter of lust, but of psychological warfare against the city, demoralising those who remained and demonstrating dominance. The Assyrians actually left art that celebrated these practices. Yet in the extensive body of literature that we have received from ancient Israel there is no mention of this as part of how Israel conducted war. Despite the real ethical problems that remain in this text, God is restricting the worst of human impulses in at least four ways. First, sexual activity is intended for marriage, and is not meant to be weaponised against one's enemies. Second, instead of using rape on the battlefield to satisfy lust, a man must wait one month before he can have sex with the woman he has captured. Third, he can't merely have sex with her; he has to marry her. Finally, if he doesn't want to remain married to her, he must not enslave her or sell her. He has to let her go, free, as if she is any other Israelite woman who is divorced by her husband.

By this law, God showed concern for captured, foreign, sexually abused women, and he called his people to act differently from surrounding nations. If sometimes God did not force his people to make as much of a change as we might have wished, it is because he knows that people can only be pushed so far or so fast. God wades through the mire of our violent, sinful world to act in defence of those who are defenceless and to call his people to do the same.

2 Punishment and dignity

Rebellion was considered a terrible crime in the ancient world and nearly always resulted in death. Either following that death, or as part of it, those who had rebelled would frequently be taken and hung on trees or impaled on a pole. They would be left there for days or even weeks, to rot and to be eaten by scavengers. The purpose wasn't only to shame and demean the dead individual, but to serve as a warning to the living: 'Don't let this happen to you.'

We have evidence from ancient art of the ubiquity of this practice. But as with the former law about war rape, God allows this practice only in a very limited sense. A person may only be left hanging on a tree until the evening, and then they must be buried. No long-term exposure. No opportunity for scavengers to eat the body. No watching it or smelling it rot in the hot sun. Here, I think, is why, in Genesis 1:26, God says, 'Let us make man in our image, after our likeness.' A lot of debate has gone on through the years about what 'image' means: Creativity? Empathy? Intellect? Spiritual sense? But we miss what follows '. . . and let them have dominion'. The word *tselem* means 'image', but our Bibles usually translate it another way, 'idol'. Idols in the ancient world were made as representations of the gods. But the only 'image' of Yahweh that the Israelites had was each other. To desecrate a body is to desecrate Yahweh's image, his earthly representative.

The law in Deuteronomy 25:1–3 has similar aims. Corporal punishment was common in the ancient world for many offences, and this law restricts the worst abuses of that practice, in three ways. First, the very context is judicial. Corporal punishment was not meant to allow for some sort of vengeful justice wrought by a mob. Second, that 40 lashes is a maximum implies that most penalties would be well short of that. Finally, the reasoning, again, is that of human dignity, this time based not directly on the image of God, but on the issue of family. This man who is to be beaten is a brother, so far as the covenant is concerned. And perhaps that reframing of the situation is meant to cause the one who would take a brother to court to consider how he may be treated as family and how reconciliation, rather than retribution, might be the wiser and kinder course.

3 'But what was she wearing?'

Deuteronomy 22:23–27

One of the laws most often deemed unjust in Deuteronomy is this two-part law. It is important to note that unlike a modern western couple's engagement, betrothal was as binding as marriage, which is why adultery with a betrothed woman was treated like adultery with a married woman (Deuteronomy 22:23–24). But it is deeply troubling to many that the apparent response to a betrothed woman having sex in the city was apparently automatic and unquestioning condemnation as adultery if she did not call for help. But, people ask, what if she was threatened? What if she was knocked out? What if he held a knife to her throat? These are important, real-world questions. But the way biblical law functioned, I do not believe that there was any category for 'guilty on a technicality'. The scenarios in case law were intentionally generic. The complexities of real life then became extenuating circumstances for which the judges would have to account. The law contains the simplest version of the issue. If a couple is caught having sex in the city and the woman is betrothed and she seems to offer no resistance, she should be treated as an adulteress, unless there is reason to indicate otherwise. 'Crying out' likely refers only to the most straightforward form of resistance.

I would suggest that the second part of this law indicates that the judiciary was to err on the side of kindness towards the woman and belief in her story, regardless of where the incident occurs. There is no guidance given in the second part of the law to distinguish between rape and adultery. But the default was to assume that the woman was innocent. The default was to assume that she tried to escape or seek help, but couldn't. Putting these two laws together strongly suggests that the woman would be given the benefit of the doubt, even in the first scenario.

Care for victims of violent crime and sexual violation is absolutely essential. Believing women – and men – when they report sexual harassment or sexual assault should be our default, while still being sure to investigate such matters carefully. Victim blaming remains a problem and likely will continue to be so because it is easy to feel less responsibility for a victim if we can blame them for their suffering. Scripture does not tell us to ask sufferers if they deserve their suffering, but rather to be caring and compassionate to all who suffer the effects of violence and sin.

120

4 Refugees

Deuteronomy 23:7-8, 15-16

Biblical law is incredibly clear that the nations surrounding Israel were spiritually dangerous to them. The moral and spiritual practices of those nations, and the injustice that so often characterised their government, was seen as a corrupting influence that had to be removed from Israel's own land and avoided in their interactions with their neighbours.

It would have been understandable, then, if Israel's immigration and refugee policy was to 'close ranks' and prohibit any non-Israelites from citizenship. And yet, that's not at all the case. Certainly some nations, such as Ammon and Moab, as mentioned in Deuteronomy 23:3-6, were considered too spiritually dangerous. (Though the inclusion of the book of Ruth and her story is a noteworthy exception.) But some others could be welcomed over time. Edom is perhaps an understandable choice, as the people group closest to Israel, though the ongoing animosity between the two nations may have made it a somewhat unlikely event. Much more surprising is Egypt. Despite the slavery, and God's mighty acts of judgement against them, he reminds them of the beginning of the story: that Israel had been a stranger in Egypt. Egypt had made space for Israel, however badly that ended, and so Israel was always to make space for Egypt.

But what is described here is a slow process, over decades, perhaps more an acknowledgement of assimilation than the welcoming of foreigners. For a wholehearted welcoming of the other, we turn to Deuteronomy 23:15-16. This law is notable because it makes no requirements. A slave escaped from another nation is not asked his people group, or made to wait any amount of time, or made to go to a certain place, but is instead welcomed and allowed to settle anywhere. While surely he would come to be expected to follow Israel's laws, this law is not concerned first with his holiness or the threat he might pose to the community, but only first with making him safe and securing his position in society.

As we consider the profound international disasters of our time, resulting in people fleeing from any number of countries, perhaps we should consider that anything less than full-throated welcoming of refugees cannot claim to be derived from Judeo-Christian values.

5 No covenant without consequences

It is a well-established position that Deuteronomy is structured in the matter of an ancient Near Eastern suzerain-vassal covenant or treaty. This treaty form made for peace between kings and their subject states, and stated what was required for a vassal to remain in the good graces of the overlord (suzerain). The covenant would conclude with blessings for obedience and curses for disobedience.

We tend to be very comfortable with the first of those and much less comfortable with the second. Many people memorise the beatitudes, but far fewer memorize the woes (Luke 6:20–26). And of course, ours is a faith of mercy and grace and blessing. It is right and good that we spend a majority of our time celebrating the goodness of God as manifested through his blessings. But we must not ignore the goodness of God as manifested through his judgement.

God is not just if he blesses his people for their faithfulness, but ignores them in their disobedience. God is not good if he keeps only his promises to give good things, but not his promises to judge evil. Wedding vows and ordination vows are meaningless if those who make them cannot be held to account. Not even the most secular modern contract is absent of penalties for failure to meet the terms of the contract. There is no covenant without consequences.

The ritual of the tribes pronouncing blessings and curses opposite each other that is described in this chapter was meant to happen in the promised land. That was likely meant to provide more weight to the curses for unfaithfulness. While Israel was already the covenant people of God, how much worse would covenant unfaithfulness be once Israel was in the land, having finally received all that God had promised to their ancestors?

Many of the curses pertain to laws that would have been more difficult to enforce. Two of the laws specifically state things done in secret (Deuteronomy 27:15, 24). But many of the others, including the laws about dishonesty and illicit sexual relationships, are matters that are easy to conceal and hard to prove. The curses therefore also provide a way to remind the people that even when human justice may be escaped, divine justice cannot be.

6 Sing them over again to me

Deuteronomy 31:9–13

One of the three major festivals that Israel celebrated each year was the Feast of Booths – or as I like to think of it, Family Camp. Once each year, they were to build themselves a little temporary shelter and live in it for a week to remind them of their nation's formative years as wilderness nomads. But every seven years, there was an added piece to it: the law was to be read. Good writing materials were expensive and literacy rates quite low. Parts of it were surely memorised and it was taught through the ministry of the Levites, but there were probably very few people who had regular opportunity to hear the entirety of the law. So once every seven years, the people were to gather not only for Family Camp but also to hear the whole law read: not only God's commands, but the entire record of his covenant relationship with his people.

The interesting part is with which feast they experienced this Sabbath year event. The reading of the law first happened in the wilderness, while the people were landless nomads. The Feast of Booths recreated the wilderness experience; the reading of the law adds another layer to that return to their roots. They would get, as much as possible, a sense of what their ancestors experienced in that time that they were on the verge of claiming the promises of God.

It is good for us to go back to the beginning now and again: to recall and re-experience God's good work in our lives. Often we do this when we commemorate anniversaries of various sorts. It happens more sporadically when we witness a baptism. And hopefully, it happens each week as we hear the gospel preached. We never lose our need to hear the good news of God's work: the work that has saved us, that is saving us and that will save us in the end.

Sing them over again to me,
Wonderful words of life;
Let me more of their beauty see,
Wonderful words of life;
Words of life and beauty
Teach me faith and duty.
Beautiful words, wonderful words,
Wonderful words of life.

Philip Bliss (1838–76)

Guidelines

As we've looked through the laws of Deuteronomy and the selection of legal issues that feature in the curses in Deuteronomy 27, it is striking that nearly all the requirements of the great king in Deuteronomy are concerned not with doing good directly to the king, but to his subjects, and especially those of his subjects who are most vulnerable. Issues of human dignity, victims' rights and immigrants and refugees have been concerns throughout human history, and in the law that God gave to Israel, he attempts to use the privilege that he has to set the standard not for selfish ends but to ensure that his people will be good to others. Psalm 146:9 says, 'The Lord watches over the sojourners; he upholds the widow and the fatherless, but the way of the wicked he brings to ruin.' In Isaiah 1:17, God calls his people to imitate him by doing the same.

Throughout all of the law and the prophets and the writings, God tells his people to imitate him by leveraging their power and privilege to care for the vulnerable, just as he has done. That should lead us to very uncomfortable questions, both personally and in our churches. Have we made safe spaces for the abused in our assemblies? Have I pressed a house key into the hand of a woman who I think may be abused and told her to use it, day or night? Have the newcomers in my neighbourhood received a loaf of homemade bread and my mobile number? Have we as a church held a picnic and invited the Muslim immigrant neighbourhood that has sprung up blocks from the church building? And, most of all, do we beg our Lord in prayer to give us the eyes to see needs of every sort and the courage and compassion to meet them in healthy and holistic ways?

FURTHER READING

Daniel Block, *Deuteronomy* (Zondervan, 2012).

Daniel Block, *The Triumph of Grace: Literary and theological studies in Deuteronomy and Deuteronomic themes* (Cascade, 2017).

Jen Pollock Michel, *A Habit Called Faith: 40 days in the Bible to find and follow Jesus* (Baker, 2021).

Christopher J. H. Wright, *Deuteronomy* (Baker, 2012, new edition).

2 Peter

Michael Parsons

The apostle Peter may or may not have written the letter accredited to him in the canon of scripture. It's possible that someone other than Jesus' disciple wrote it, claiming the apostle's authority. We'll leave that conundrum to the experts to discuss. Either way, this epistle is written with deep pastoral concern and biblical insight. For the purposes of these notes, I will assume Petrine authorship.

However, it is true that the second letter of Peter is not the easiest part of the New Testament to get our heads around. With a whole chapter on false teachers worming their way into people's lives and another about the end of the world at Christ's dramatic second coming, we might be forgiven for giving this short, three-chapter epistle a miss! But, in fact, we'd lose out on a great deal.

Peter, writing to Christian believers he'd probably never met, but with whom he felt a spiritual bond of fellowship in Christ, exhorts them to heed his words over against those 'cleverly devised stories' (1:16) that might take them away from their Saviour and their faith. In this context, he speaks of divine power, of growth in grace, of the authenticity of the gospel, of the coming day of the Lord and of the divine gracious patience that all may be saved. These are foundational themes on which to prayerfully reflect.

The following notes merely scratch the surface of this wonderful letter. But as you read them, with the biblical text, perhaps you could consider your own situation – your faith, your grasp of the gospel's truth. You may like to pray that the Holy Spirit would apply Peter's words, his ancient exhortations, to your contemporary faith. What might Peter say to you and to your church today?

Unless otherwise stated Bible quotations are from the TNIV.

1 Make every effort

This is the apostle's second letter to scattered Christians. The first dealt with problems from outside the church, notably persecution. In contrast, this letter deals with problems within the church, particularly false teachers seeking to win over converts to their erroneous thinking.

The conventional form of address is used. He says that he is not only an apostle of Jesus Christ, but his servant too. The designation of servant, used in this way, was one of honour and privilege. Peter probably has in mind others who had gone before: Moses, Jesus. It implies a calling, a task – obedience.

Peter writes to those with faith, those loved and called by God through the sacrificial work of Jesus, who he designates 'God', 'Saviour', 'Christ' (v. 1). He speaks of 'grace and peace' – a conventional phrase, Christianised. Believers receive grace and peace through 'knowledge of God and of Jesus our Lord' (v. 2). Look up the idea of knowing God in the Bible, particularly in 1 John, perhaps, and see what that entails. You'll see that it's never simply cerebral; it's profoundly personal and includes the response of our lives to that knowledge.

He adds that this personal knowledge brings the gift of all that disciples need to live godly lives (v. 3): including, but not exclusively, faith, goodness, knowledge, self-control, perseverance, godliness, mutual affection, love (vv. 5–7). God's provisions for living in a corrupt world (v. 4) are complete. There's nothing lacking. Why not reflect on your own life with these gifts in mind. How are they evidenced in your life?

There is a need to continue to grow in the likeness of Jesus, to be genuine disciples of the Lord, to live in a way that is pleasing to God. 'Make every effort,' exhorts Peter (v. 10). Though the Lord has given us everything we need (v. 3), it's still necessary to make a determined effort to be godly, pleasing to him. Or, better, it's *because* God has given us everything!

2 It bears repetition

The main purpose of this letter is to warn against false teachers in the church (2:1). In contrast to their erroneous teaching, Peter seeks to convince the believers that his gospel is genuine and authoritative. Two things are foundational to this argument: his own experience and the prophetic message.

Peter's own experience of being present at Christ's glorious transfiguration proves that he isn't simply following 'cleverly devised stories' (v. 16). He was one of a very few eyewitnesses of the divine majesty on that occasion. *This happened*, says Peter. This is fact, truth, history. He was present. He knows. He saw it, he heard it (vv. 16, 18). For us today, too, experience is important to our faith. What experiences have encouraged you to believe more firmly in God? Consider these, reflecting on the Lord's goodness.

Peter remarks that they also have 'the prophetic message' – the 'completely reliable' Old Testament scriptures. Employing Old Testament imagery about the word of God, he states that that it was 'a light shining in a dark place' (v. 19). What place has the Bible had in your Christian discipleship? Do you read the Old Testament as God's reliable word?

So, on this double foundation – his own experience of Christ and the prophetic word – the apostle writes against the false teachers in the church. He can write with certainty because he knows that what he says is true. It has the authority of God about it.

Therefore, Peter wants to 'remind [them] of these things… to refresh [their] memory' (vv. 12–13). He is determined that they 'will always be able to remember these things' (v. 15). Such is their importance! They know these truths already, but they are so significant for Christian living and for standing firm in the faith that Peter doesn't mind repeating them. And perhaps we should never mind being reminded of things we already know either. Truth bears repetition.

We might, today, apply this to the New Testament writings as well, of course. We would do well to pay attention to it, says the apostle. It leads us into light. It takes us out of the darkness of the fallen world. Ultimately, it shows us Jesus our Saviour.

3 Beware, false teachers!

Chapter two of Peter's letter is about the danger of false teachers in the church. He makes the point that just as there were false prophets among the godly prophets of Israel, so there are false teachers amid the righteous teachers in the fellowship. This has always been the case (v. 1). And so it is, sadly, today.

The apostle asserts that these false teachers already stand condemned (v. 3), but it is worth looking at what their characteristics are. Look through the description that Peter gives of these false teachers. How can we, as leaders or teachers in the church, guard against falling into their trap? Perhaps you could reflect on where you presently stand on this matter.

The Old Testament examples Peter uses are graphic. Those condemned, judged, angels being sent to hell, the ungodly being drowned in the flood, Sodom and Gomorrah razed to the ground. And those delivered: 'Noah, a preacher of righteousness', protected (v. 5), 'Lot, a righteous man', rescued (v. 7). He concludes that 'the Lord knows how to rescue the godly and to hold the unrighteous for… judgement' (v. 9).

Is truth important? Is judgement serious? Does God care about such things? The apostle assures us that these things matter – even today in a postmodern world that generally eschews 'truth'. The false things that these teachers impart are leading men and women astray from the gospel of Jesus Christ.

The sobering thought about these teachers is that they have been believers. They had received grace. They had known the truth. Now, Peter insists 'they are worse off at the end than they were at the beginning' (v. 20) – hence the proverbs at the end of the chapter.

Peter speaks into a specific situation, of course. However, what he says has relevance to us today – whether we are teachers or not, but particularly if we are teachers. What do we believe (and teach)? Is it the truth of the word of God? Are we careful in how we read and use the scriptures? Or have we become a little careless through familiarity?

4 The Lord's patience

2 Peter 3:1–9

Peter writes to remind believers of the message that came from 'holy prophets' – completely reliable (1:19), spoken somehow from God (1:21); to recall, too, the apostolic teaching originating from Jesus (v. 2). This message appears to be about the last days, the end of this world, the final deliverance of God's people. Peter, then, picks out one or two emphases of that instruction.

First, and importantly (v. 3, 'above all'), scoffers will come in the last days. The New Testament thinks of 'the last days' not as the final few, but rather those days ushered in by the resurrection of Christ and until his return. Some unbelievers (not all) will ridicule the truth; they deride the idea of the second coming of Christ (v. 4). How do you answer such cynicism? How do you seek to persuade others of this truth?

Second, we are encouraged to realise the Lord's ability to fulfil his promise. After all, by God's word the whole of creation came into being (v. 5), by divine fiat the world of Noah's day was destroyed (v. 6). It's the same divine word that sustains the world until judgement (v. 7). The creating word; the judging word; the recreating word – all assured and certain because this is God's word! Why not reflect on the word of God and what that means? How significant is it to see it in several aspects?

Third, we are reminded to remember that 'with the Lord a day is like a thousand years, and a thousand years are like a day' (v. 8). Scoffers measure the credibility of God's promise of Christ's return by the apparently interminable slowness of its fulfilment (as some of us no doubt sometimes do, too). But the apostle is adamant. The Lord's desire is that everyone might come to repentance, 'not wanting anyone to perish' (v. 9) – and if that means patient 'delay', then so be it. It's a mark of tremendous grace on his part. Does our witnessing show the same remarkable patience? How might this be seen in practise?

The apostle wrote this to stimulate 'wholesome thinking' – healthy, sensible, helpful thinking (v. 1). There was and there still is some irrational thinking about the Lord's coming, incoherent of the gospel and of the Lord's love. Peter simply reminds us that Jesus Christ *will* return again – that's as certain as God's word. His patience and the apparent 'delay' give humanity time to turn to him. You might turn this thought into prayer for those you know – and for those you don't.

5 What kind of people?

Having spoken of the certainty of the Lord's second coming, the apostle Peter now asserts that he will come when we least expect him – picking up conventional themes and images (see 1 Thessalonians 5:1–3). He also stresses the completeness of the event (v. 10) – a thorough, meticulous and comprehensive cleansing and renewal at the powerful coming of Christ.

Peter applies this with a pointed question: if this is the case, 'what kind of people ought you to be?' (v. 11). It would be difficult to be more direct! Why not reflect on this as you answer the question for yourself? Does the fact that the whole of creation is going to be renewed at Christ's future coming affect how we live in the present? Does it have an ecological application?

Peter speaks of looking forward to that day, of somehow speeding its coming (v. 12). We look forward to it because it will flag the end of this present evil age; a new one will dawn, 'a new heaven and a new earth, where righteousness dwells' (v. 13; see also Revelation 21:4; 22:3) – everything brand new!

Looking at this passage, is our focus far too often on the present time and not enough on the gracious promises of God for the future – our future? How might his gracious promises for the future change your perspective on things?

An important caveat, though: we don't want to be so heavenly-minded that we're no earthly use. That's certainly not Peter's point. Jesus involved himself with the 'world', with sinners and tax-collectors. The church has always had a social concern and an active interest in justice, especially for the poor and the marginalised – and this is right. It's part of the godliness and holiness that the apostle mentions in verse 11.

Indeed, let's go further and say that, knowing that the day of the Lord is certainly coming, we *must* be involved graciously with the world around us. All of this is going to be consumed by holy fire at the second coming. Today, then, is the day of salvation. That final consummation of all of God's promises should recommend action now, today.

Since everything will be destroyed in this way, what kind of people ought we to be?

6 Be at peace with God

2 Peter 3:14–16

The apostle speaks of the recipients of the letter as 'dear friends' ('beloved'), alluding to the close bond they have in Christ. In chapter 3 alone this expression occurs four times (vv. 1, 8, 14, 17). He writes out of love for them, out of concern – especially as some may have only just come to faith in Jesus Christ (see 2:18). This suggests that those of us who are longer in the faith should support those who are newer to it. Do we pray for them? Do we encourage them? Have they become 'dear friends'?

The apostle exhorts his readers to make the effort 'to be found spotless, blameless' (v. 14). Work at it, he says. Make it the major concern of your lives. Exert energy in its pursuit. How does this exhortation speak to your life on a day-to-day basis?

They are also to be at peace with God (v. 14). They have peace with him already, of course – that comes through faith in Jesus Christ (see Romans 5:1), but the apostle encourages them to continue in this peace, this fellowship, through prayer and openness to the Spirit, through godliness and confession.

Peter has already warned his readers (v. 17), so he exhorts them to 'be on [their] guard' against lawless people. If they're not careful, they might 'fall from [their] secure position'. Of course, the foundation of their faith is secure: built on the work of apostles and prophets, and Jesus Christ as the chief cornerstone (Ephesians 2:20; see 1 Peter 2:5). That is not in question. But their footing on that foundation might be if they get carried away by error. You might reflect on whether you are being 'careful' in this respect. What does that look like for you? How are you building on that foundation?

The apostle encourages them to 'grow in the grace and knowledge of our Lord and Saviour Jesus Christ' (v. 18). This is the antidote to falling from grace! Let your experience of Christ continue to mature. Learn to know him more. What might this mean for us on a daily basis? Peter fittingly concludes with doxology, praise to Christ.

Guidelines

Among other things, we have underlined the following key areas from 2 Peter:

- The Christian life should be one of determined effort. The Lord has given salvation in Jesus Christ, but Peter urges his readers to 'make every effort' (3:14) in their following of him. We have everything we need in Christ. However, we are exhorted to 'add to our faith' the virtues that will keep our lives from being fruitless and ineffective, and to be found spotless when he returns. That doesn't always sit comfortably with our busy lives, nor with the prevailing church ethos. What might we do to make sure we don't stumble and to maintain a good witness in the world?

- There will always be false teachers in the church. Peter reminds us that the false teachers he writes against were once members of the church. They have now left the fellowship. But Peter stresses that they are condemned already! This is a solemn warning to those of us who teach in any way in the church. Care needs to be taken if we want to present gospel truth: care in engaging with scripture, care in teaching it and care in living it.

- The word of God, and all its implications, has authority. The writer speaks of the creative word, the divine spoken words on the sacred mountain, the prophetic word, the word of recreation, of judgement, the words of promise – all words of utmost authority. How has the word of God, in its different forms, perhaps, formed us into the believers we are today? Do we give faithful credence to the word of God, despite the world's resolve to follow 'cleverly devised stories' (1:16) of their own?

- The Lord is gracious and patient. Peter reminds us that the Lord is patient with the world that seems determined to go its own way. How might we share in that gracious patience in the situations and circumstances in which we find ourselves? Is the church for the world, as the Lord is? What witness to Christ's love do we offer those for whom the Lord waits?

Prayerfully reflect on your responses within the context of your own life and Christian community. The Lord bless you as you do that.

FURTHER READING

Peter Davids, *The Letters of 2 Peter and Jude* (Eerdmans, 2006).
Paul Gardner, 1 and 2 Peter and Jude (Christian Focus, 2013).
Dick Lucas and Christopher Green, *The Message of 2 Peter and Jude* (IVP, 2021).

Philippians

Rosalee Velloso Ewell

Paul's arrival in Philippi was very dramatic. During one night in Troas (modern-day Türkiye), he had a dream of a man from Macedonia begging him for help (Acts 16). So he sailed to Philippi, the main city in Macedonia. Instead of finding the man from his dream, he encountered various women who gathered by the river to pray. Paul spoke to them about Jesus and later freed a slave girl from a spirit of divination, upsetting her owners who then dragged Paul and his friend Silas before the authorities, had them severely beaten and thrown in prison. There was an earthquake that night that would have permitted an escape, but instead Paul and his friends stayed in prison, which led to the conversion of the jailer. This was the beginning of the first church in Europe. It was also the start of a deep friendship and partnership in the gospel between Paul and those Christians in Philippi.

Some say Philippians is Paul's swansong, but Peruvian scholar, Pedro Arana, argues that it is Paul's call to subversion! Philippians paints a picture of the world through the lens of God's providential care for all God's creation and invites each person to live in this upside-down kingdom inaugurated by Jesus, God's Son.

At the time of writing Philippians, Paul was in prison in Ephesus; he had upset both the religious and civil leaders and his future was extremely uncertain. Yet whether he was to live or be executed (see 1:21), he exudes joy and gratitude as he writes to his friends, encouraging them in the daily tasks of following Jesus. Paul's words to them are words for Christians today – he invites the Philippians to 'shine like stars in the world' (2:15). This is God's invitation to us today.

Unless otherwise stated, Bible quotations are from the NRSV. Author references are to works in the 'Further reading' list.

1 Not a trivial joy

Philippians 1:1–11

Paul begins this letter with a standard greeting: 'Grace to you and peace from God.' But behind the common format there are glimpses of themes that will reappear in the letter, along with a general tone of love and familiarity with his readers. Unlike other churches started by Paul, such as Corinth, the Philippians do not question Paul's authority as an apostle of Christ, so stating it here is unnecessary.

Paul and Timothy's self-identification as servants of Christ Jesus (v. 1) hints at the themes of belonging and citizenship that will appear later on. In the ancient world, a slave would be identified with his or her owner. Paul is imprisoned by the Roman authorities, but he makes clear that he is a slave of Christ and it is to Jesus that he belongs and whom he serves. There is no other loyalty or identity. Furthermore, Paul asserts that the Philippians share in this identity and in the gospel for which Paul is imprisoned (v. 5, v. 7). As Stephen Fowl explains, as a slave of Christ, Paul 'is accountable to his master, who will evaluate his service' (Fowl, p. 17). Therefore Paul is a gentle pastor, indicating in this letter a series of themes and habits that the Philippians need to develop if they, too, are going to be slaves of Christ. All such attitudes and behaviours are possible because Christ himself took on the form of a slave (2:7).

Paul is joyful in his memories of the Philippians and in his continued prayers for them (vv. 3–4). This seems contradictory, given Paul's current context of imprisonment and the fact that he received one of his most brutal beatings when he was first in Philippi (Acts 16:22–24). Yet this is no trivial joy nor is he making light of suffering. Rather, Paul is absolutely convinced that it is God who is at work in him and in his readers, setting them aside as a holy people ('saints' in v. 1), overflowing with love, wisdom and knowledge of what it means to live in a Christlike manner (vv. 9–11). Tom Wright highlights the image of God who is both 'the finisher' and 'the beginner' of the work of grace (Wright, p. 83). Through Paul's testimony, God started an amazing work in Philippi and they can all be joyful and confident that God will finish that work, even when circumstances seem dire.

Paul and the Philippians are in partnership for the gospel, with all the financial, emotional and relational characteristics of real collaboration. Their partnership and belonging to one another is only possible because of Christ, and so Paul will spend the rest of this joyful letter examining the implications of the work God is doing in Paul himself and in the Philippian church.

2 Life or death: which would you choose?

Philippians 1:12–26

We are familiar with governments (or others with power and money) trying to hush up a scandal. And we know how 'influencers' or news items leaked to the media can change public opinion very quickly. In the absence of social media and quick news outlets that expose a scandal, Paul's letter aims for a similar outcome – to encourage the Philippians that even in prison, Paul is not silenced and that the gospel he preaches is actually proclaimed with more boldness and volume.

The beheading of 21 Coptic Christians by ISIS in 2015 was intended to strike fear and retreat into Christians everywhere, especially those in Egypt and the Middle East. But the faith of those martyrs and the courageous witness of the church resulted in the opposite effect: a renewal of a bold Christian witness and an affirmation that only Jesus is Lord. The God of whom Paul writes in this letter is the Lord of life and death, so that even when opponents of the gospel try to stir up more trouble (1:15a), they are actually helping to spread the good news about Jesus (1:18).

Paul paints a picture of how one lives (and dies) through the lens of Jesus' lordship. This results in a vision of the world and a way of understanding one's own life that Paul wishes to pass on to the Philippians – 'one of the aims of presenting an account of his circumstances [imprisonment and persecution]… is so that they [the Philippians] can begin to develop similar patterns of perception, judgement and action for themselves' (Fowl, p. 36).

Part of 1:19 is a quote from the book of Job (Job 13:16). Though the Philippians might not have heard this Old Testament echo in Paul's letter, it highlights for us the confidence Paul has in God's justice. Just as Job knows he will be vindicated by God, so Paul urges the Philippians to see their own situation (and that of Paul) in light of God's sovereignty over every circumstance. This includes how they see life and death.

'Bodily actions… display elements of a person's character' (Fowl, p. 48). Paul is torn – on one hand he affirms that to die would bring him into a more intimate relationship with Jesus, but on the other he knows there is work still to be done (1:21–24). Thus, every day of Paul's life (and ours) must be lived in a way that makes death itself display God's glory and salvation.

3 Reimagining unity

Philippians 1:27—2:11

There is a common saying, 'We are better together…' In this letter, one could say that Paul ends the saying with 'even in suffering'. The spotlight shifts in 1:27 from Paul's own sufferings to the persecution and challenges that those Christians in Philippi are up against. As their pastor, he longs to be with them to encourage and help them understand and live out their Christian faith in a hostile environment. They must order their common life in such a way that displays the work of Christ in them and that follows Christ's own selfless path. Similar to Paul's own imprisonment, their standing firm together in Christ will shame their persecutors and display God's victory.

Jesus' prayer in John 17:21, 'that they all may be one', is often cited at church gatherings and conferences on church unity with the aim and prayer of overcoming the many divisions that exist among us. Paul echoes this prayer here but insists that it is not unity simply for unity's sake. Rather, it is unity that displays the character of our witness. The world is watching! Your oppressors are watching! Will they see Christ in your common life? This is the urgent challenge Paul puts to his readers.

Some things are best expressed through music or poetry. One such example is 2:5–11 – it is one of the most studied passages of the New Testament. The apostle's aim to give the Philippians a new lens through which to see their contexts and to discern how to live in a Christlike manner reaches its climax in this text. God's kingdom turns the world and its values upside down. The creator and ruler of the universe is not the emperor with all his military might, but the Son of God who took on the form of a slave and died on the cross (2:7–8). 'Only when we grasp this do we see… how deeply subversive [and] countercultural was Paul's gospel message concerning Jesus' (Wright, p. 101).

The Philippians and the church today must learn to put others before ourselves (2:3) because ours is a 'God who is known most clearly when he abandons his rights for the sake of the world' (Wright, p. 104). Thus, to share in the Spirit (2:1) and to have the same mind that was in Christ (2:2, 5), entails a reimagination of how one sees the world and lives in unity with others.

4 Who wants to be a star?

Philippians 2:12—3:1

It should not surprise us that after such a beautiful poem about Jesus' incarnation, crucifixion and exaltation, Paul hopes that his readers are duly inspired and ready for more advice on the implications of following the crucified Lord. He starts off this section with an extraordinary promise that echoes what he said in 1:6 – 'It is God who is at work in you, enabling you both to will and to work for his good pleasure' (2:13). What an amazing thought: the same God who is creator and ruler, who became incarnate in Jesus, is at work in you!

This promise is followed by another promise, but a conditional one: if you do A, B and C, you will shine like stars (2:15). Who does not want to be a star? But again, our common worldviews are turned upside down and our visions of stardom are shattered. To shine like a star means attending to the little things, to how we talk to one another, how we talk about others, how we behave in our day-to-day tasks. Remember that earlier in the letter Paul paid special attention to how the Philippians ordered their common life. Living according to the gospel is countercultural precisely because it means seeing the world and all our priorities through the lens of Jesus. Even in their suffering and in Paul's own desperate situation, if they hold fast to the word of God, they will be able to rejoice (2:17), knowing that God is completing the work of salvation in them.

The unity of which Paul wrote earlier extends beyond those immediately in Philippi to other Christians who are also 'coworkers' in the gospel cause (2:25). Timothy and Epaphroditus are two such examples. They demonstrate in their self-sacrificial love towards Paul and to the church at Philippi that it matters a great deal who our friends are. Timothy had been in Philippi with Paul. Epaphroditus was the messenger sent by the Philippians bearing gifts for Paul. Epaphroditus had nearly died trying to carry out his important mission, so part of Paul's desire to send him back to his community is so that they can hear first-hand how important that gift was for Paul and to see their friend in good health. Together they can rejoice both in his healing and in the fact that they all share in the labours of the gospel.

5 A different kind of citizenship

In contrast to the faithful witnesses of Timothy and Epaphroditus, Paul shifts his focus to warning the Philippians about those so-called friends who could lure them away from Christ. In other regions where Paul had founded a church, such as Galatia, the communities had been infiltrated by Jewish Christians who, unlike Paul, argued that the Gentile believers were not fully Christian unless they also submitted to the laws of Israel, especially circumcision. Though this had not happened yet in Philippi, Paul was worried that it could and so he emphasises – 'Beware... beware... beware!' (3:2).

The danger of these troublemakers in the churches was multilayered: (i) they caused divisions among the Christians, which goes against Paul's emphasis on the unity that is needed for the integrity of the church's witness; (ii) they preached a distorted gospel that boasted in their own achievements 'in the flesh', which goes against the gift of God's grace and the importance of understanding that God (not the law) is both the beginner and the finisher of the work of faith; (iii) their obsession with 'the flesh' made them just like all the other pagan peoples; (iv) they shifted the spotlight away from Jesus to their own identity as descendants of Abraham according to the law. Paul argues (3:4–6) that he, above all, has reason to boast in his heritage and yet in Christ, he was given a new identity.

It is through Christ's death and resurrection (2:9–10) that the Philippians and Christians of all times are given new identities and called to a different kind of citizenship. When asked the question: 'Where are you from?', the answer Paul wants us all to give is 'from Christ!' To affirm that our citizenship is in Jesus is a political statement and one that had already got Paul and the Philippians into a lot of trouble. The powers of this world, both then and now, do not look kindly on those who affirm that only Jesus is Lord.

Having a 'heavenly citizenship' (3:20) is not only about a future, spiritual hope. It is a concrete reality in the present. Hence Paul's emphasis that the Philippians must order their common lives in such a way that sets them apart, holy and blameless, displaying the love they have for one another and for Jesus, even in their sufferings. Theirs is an embodied faith that shows to those around them that indeed they have a different kind of citizenship.

6 A 'thank you' card

Throughout the letter, Paul has made a case for how and why the Philippians need to develop a way of seeing, judging and living in the world that is like Jesus and that witnesses to the upside-down ways that God has set forth. 'Paul both advocates and displays a set of habits and dispositions that will help the Philippians in their struggle to live faithfully before God in a context that is hostile to them' (Fowl, p. 176). This way of living only makes sense because of the story of Christ (2:5–11). Now, towards the end of his letter, he applies this advice to some particular examples within the Philippian community (vv. 2–3). His admonishments to them are given in the context of joy and filled with confidence that they will indeed hold fast to the word of life, which in turn results in a beautiful common life and witness. The character of that common life is honourable, just, pure, pleasing, commendable, excellent and worthy of praise (v. 8). All these lovely characteristics are the outcome of learning to be faithful to Christ, even, or especially, in the little things. For the Philippians and for us today, it is about learning to be servants and to regard all others as more important than ourselves. This is the picture Paul hopes his letter has painted for them and given them the assurance that this is the world ordered by God (v. 9).

To conclude his letter, Paul returns to one of the main reasons for writing: to say a huge 'thank you!' for the gift the Philippians sent him via Epaphroditus. As Tom Wright explains, prisoners in the ancient world did not receive food or other supplies from their captors and so they relied on gifts and support from friends (Wright, p. 84). While Paul is clear that he has learned to be content and to praise God no matter what the circumstances (vv. 11–13), he acknowledges this gift alongside others that he has received from Philippi and is deeply grateful for the way they have supported him from the very beginning of his European ministry. Finally, he shows how their gift is also a sign of their partnership in the gospel. Providing for Paul becomes a gift pleasing to God (v. 18) and witnesses to the deep sharing between Paul and the Philippians in both their joys and their sufferings for the gospel. Together, all this is for the glory of God.

Guidelines

- In a culture shaped by social media and where faith is often seen as a private matter, how does Paul's emphasis on our common life challenge Christians today to reconsider how our lives *together* witness to Jesus Christ?
- The famous passage of Philippians 2:5–11 shows that Christ's glory is actually to be found in his humiliation as a slave. What work, what aspirations for greatness and recognition must we give up in order to follow Christ faithfully?

FURTHER READING

Stephen E. Fowl, *Philippians* (Eerdmans, 2005).

Tom Wright, *Paul for Everyone: The prison letters: Ephesians, Philippians, Colossians and Philemon* (SPCK, 2004).

Become a Friend of BRF
and give regularly to support our ministry

We help people of all ages to grow in faith

We encourage and support individual Christians and churches as they serve and resource the changing spiritual needs of communities today.

Through **Anna Chaplaincy**
we're enabling churches to provide
spiritual care to older people

Through **Living Faith**
we're nurturing faith and resourcing
life-long discipleship

Through **Messy Church**
we're helping churches to reach out
to families

Through **Parenting for Faith**
we're supporting parents as they raise
their children in the Christian faith

Our ministry is only possible because of the generous support of individuals, churches, trusts and gifts in wills.

As we look to the future and make plans, **regular donations make a huge difference** in ensuring we can both start and finish projects well.

By becoming a Friend of BRF and giving regularly to our ministry you are partnering with us in the gospel and helping change lives.

How your gift makes a difference

£2 a month — Helps us to give away **Living Faith** resources via food banks and chaplaincy services

£10 a month — Helps us to support parents and churches running the **Parenting for Faith** course

£5 a month — Helps us to support **Messy Church** volunteers and grow the wider network

£20 a month — Helps us to develop the reach of **Anna Chaplaincy** and improve spiritual care for older people

How to become a Friend of BRF

Online – set up a Direct Debit donation at brf.org.uk/donate or find out how to set up a Standing Order at brf.org.uk/friends

By post – complete and return the tear-off form opposite to 'Freepost BRF' (*no other address or stamp is needed*)

If you have any questions, or if you want to change your regular donation or stop giving in the future, do get in touch.

Contact the fundraising team

Email: giving@brf.org.uk
Tel: 01235 462305
Post: Fundraising team, BRF, 15 The Chambers, Vineyard, Abingdon OX14 3FE

Registered with
FUNDRAISING REGULATOR

Bible Reading Fellowship (BRF) is a charity (233280) and company limited by guarantee (301324), registered in England and Wales

SHARING OUR VISION – MAKING A GIFT

I would like to make a donation to support BRF.
Please use my gift for:

☐ Where it is most needed ☐ Anna Chaplaincy ☐ Living Faith
☐ Messy Church ☐ Parenting for Faith

Title	First name/initials	Surname

Address	
	Postcode

Email	

Telephone	

Signature	Date

Our ministry is only possible because of the generous support of individuals, churches, trusts and gifts in wills.

Please treat as Gift Aid donations all qualifying gifts of money made (*tick all that apply*)

giftaid it

☐ today, ☐ in the past four years, ☐ and in the future.

I am a UK taxpayer and understand that if I pay less Income Tax and/or Capital Gains Tax in the current tax year than the amount of Gift Aid claimed on all my donations, it is my responsibility to pay any difference.

☐ My donation does not qualify for Gift Aid.

Please notify BRF if you want to cancel this Gift Aid declaration, change your name or home address, or no longer pay sufficient tax on your income and/or capital gains.

You can also give online at **brf.org.uk/donate**, which reduces our administration costs, making your donation go further.

Please complete other side of form

SHARING OUR VISION – MAKING A GIFT

Please accept my gift of:

☐ £2 ☐ £5 ☐ £10 ☐ £20 Other £ ⬚

by (*delete as appropriate*):

☐ Cheque/Charity Voucher payable to 'BRF'

☐ MasterCard/Visa/Debit card/Charity card

Name on card

Card no. ⬚⬚⬚⬚ ⬚⬚⬚⬚ ⬚⬚⬚⬚ ⬚⬚⬚⬚

Expires end ⬚ M M Y Y ⬚   Security code* ⬚⬚⬚   *Last 3 digits on the reverse of the card

Signature   Date

☐ I'd like to find out about giving a regular gift to BRF.

For help or advice regarding making a gift, please contact our fundraising team +44 (0)1865 462305

Your privacy

We will use your personal data to process this transaction. From time to time we may send you information about the work of BRF that we think may be of interest to you. Our privacy policy is available at **brf.org.uk/privacy**. Please contact us if you wish to discuss your mailing preferences.

Registered with

FUNDRAISING
REGULATOR

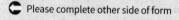 Please complete other side of form

Please return this form to 'Freepost BRF'
No other address information or stamp is needed

Bible Reading Fellowship is a charity (233280) and company limited by guarantee (301324), registered in England and Wales

GL0223

Guidelines forthcoming issue

The upcoming September issue of *Guidelines* brings us a feast of good things as we start the journey towards Advent and Christmas.

Our Advent series will kick off alongside David Spriggs, as he takes a look at the biblical witness to John the Baptist, whose extraordinary birth preceded Jesus'. Taking us up to Christmas Day, Isabelle Hamley will encourage us to think about Advent and the art of waiting, showing how different biblical characters embodied this act of waiting throughout history.

We continue a number of our series, too. Stephen Finamore rounds off his four-part series on Romans with 'Riding with Romans', which takes us through the final three chapters of the book. Andy Angel also closes out his series on Matthew as we experience once again Jesus' death, resurrection and commission to his disciples. Bill Goodman, whose series on the Psalms started in this issue, will continue with Book 2 of the Psalms (42—72), investigating God's message to the world.

Our Old Testament series for the upcoming issue is on Proverbs, with Peter Hatton unpacking this book which is sometimes accused of putting forward 'a complacent, self-satisfied morality'; instead, Peter shows us how the first nine chapters of Proverbs teach us much, especially in our 'beautiful but troubled' world. Meanwhile Leoné Martin, a new contributor, takes a deep dive into the famous John 15 passage in which Jesus gives us the beautiful metaphor of the 'true vine'.

Helen Miller (née Morris) brings us a fascinating series on images of the church in the New Testament, while Richard Martin explores Francistide to coincide with the Feast of St Francis at the beginning of October. New writer Karen O'Donnell will also bring us a week of notes on reading the Bible through the lens of trauma. Finally, Ruth Bancewicz and her team of scientists, who previously wrote about creation in *Guidelines*, return with a bioethical toolkit to help us think about how biblical principles apply to a Christian understanding of bioethics.

We hope this has whetted your appetite! May God bless your reading in the meantime.

What the Bible means to me: Sally Nash

My earliest memory of the Bible is my mum reading the story of Noah to me from the dark, floppy Bible that was a christening present from my godparents. I can feel the warmth of that experience as I recall it, even now. The Bible keeps popping up in my memories of childhood and adolescence. I loved all the Christian activities I attended: Bible stories in the park at a CSSM (now SU) holiday club, attending Young Sowers League meetings and being given a New Testament; Sunday School, Crusaders, Youth Groups. All were places where the Bible was the key focus for what we did. I am so grateful for many faithful people who accompanied me in my journey of faith.

The Bible was a source of nourishment, guidance and hope. I realised that, like Peter, I could make mistakes and Jesus was still there for me (I went to a church called St Peter's so his story was a key feature of my childhood). I am of the age that when I recite John 3:16, it is in the language of the Authorised Version. That God loves me was such a hope and encouragement to a shy, quiet child who often felt out of place.

These foundations have underpinned the rest of my life. My sense of call comes from the Bible; the way that I live is underpinned by my understanding of biblical values; and serving Jesus is the primary focus of my life. This doesn't mean that my relationship with the Bible is uncomplicated. I have had to grapple with reading the Bible as a woman. That hasn't always been easy, particularly being a childless woman, where the language of barrenness has been challenging – I am not desolate (Isaiah 54:1). I perhaps was in the early days when we realised that we would not have children and we were not going to have a miracle story to share. But my teenage years had laid the groundwork for me of trusting God, of knowing I was called to take up my cross and follow Jesus and that might not be easy.

My reading of the Bible makes it clear to me that I cannot expect an easy life. God isn't like Tinkerbell, waving a magic wand so everything is fine. Life isn't like that. Or at least it hasn't been for me, but I have had to work through the disappointments and challenges. If I couldn't, how can I tell other people about Jesus, that person I chose to follow over 50 years ago and who has led me beside both still waters and through dark valleys (Psalm 23)? I wouldn't change the choice I made to let the Bible shape my life and be my guidebook.

Recommended reading

There are no simple answers to life's challenges, so how do we integrate our most testing experiences into our faith in a way which strengthens rather than weakens it? When we are at our weakest, when we feel we most need God and yet have no idea how to talk to him, it is the Psalms which leap to our rescue. With the psalmists as our guides, we learn to draw closer to God, to hear his voice in fresh ways, and to identify what it is that troubles us. Borrowing their words, we find that we are able to articulate our most painful feelings and
walk through suffering with honesty, hope, and confidence in the God who travels beside us. *World Turned Upside Down* is an opportunity to read the Psalms differently: an invitation to embark on a new journey.

The following is an edited extract taken from a section entitled 'The elephant in the church', in Chapter 1, 'Making sense of life'.

Living in a world which has long sought to dull and deny pain, it seems natural, when we find ourselves nonetheless assailed by the slings and arrows of outrageous fortune, to turn to the church for help and support. And yet all too often we find that it isn't only our culture which urges us to believe that all is well; we bring our collective inclination to retreat into denial into the church as well. Gathering in beautiful buildings on Sundays, we sing heart-warming songs and uplifting hymns; we repeat comforting liturgical words and remind ourselves what we believe through the taking of bread and wine; we listen to a short talk and pray for those who suffer in distant places. Then we go home, taking our own doubts and difficulties with us. As biblical scholar Walter Brueggemann remarks, it's as if we believe that having faith means a refusal to acknowledge and embrace negativity; as if that would be some kind of failure. So we sing brightly and sometimes beautifully, offer one another coffee and biscuits, and go home slightly more cheerful, hoping that by pretending all is well it will become so.

And yet two things are true. The first is that one of our responsibilities as the church is to help people navigate life, not as we would like it to be, but as it actually is. And the second is that pain lies at the very heart of our faith: in encountering Jesus, we encounter a man who gathered the suffering of the world into his own suffering, who forged a path from death to life, and who through it all earned the right to offer the uniquely powerful invitation 'Come to me, all you who are weary and burdened, and I will give you rest.' Pain is the inescapable thorn in the flesh of the human condition, and an essential element in the journey of every single one of us towards God. Without pain, we cannot grow; pain is the tunnel through which we must pass if we are to reach the light at the other end. Everything depends on how we respond, and how we help others to respond. Many, at the very point when they most need to connect with God, give up on their faith altogether. Overcome by the darkness of the valley, they never reach the green pastures or rest by the refreshing waters. 'What are you going to write about?' asked an old and wise friend. 'Pain,' I replied. 'Thank God,' she said.

Every morning I read the biblical passages set for the day in the Anglican lectionary, and for the past few years I have focused on the Psalms. And in the Psalms too I have found elephants – not the grey, invisible elephants which mope their way silently through our 21st-century world and hide behind the pillars of our churches, but attention-seeking, violently coloured, lambastingly noisy ones. These elephants cannot be ignored; their trumpeting and bellowing echoes from the first psalm to the last, and they rampage with the energy of animals unrestrained in their expression of pain, of anger, of lament and finally of joy. It's said that an elephant can be heard at a distance of six miles; there is so much sheer power wrapped up in the vocalisation of an elephant that I began to pick up my Bible with a newly cautious reverence. Few people know that the elephants are there, lumbering about inside.

And yet so often we don't pray the very psalms which could most help us. 'Which psalms do I know best?', I asked myself as I began to pray my way through them. The 'nice' ones, of course. Psalm 139 probably tops the list – God made me and knows me. Psalm 46, perhaps – 'Be still, and know that I am God.' Psalm 23, of course, with its first-impression promise of green pastures. And the summer cheerfulness of Psalm 104, which sees God stretching out the heavens like a tent, renewing the face of the earth. In these psalms the elephants graze peacefully in a sunlit savannah, and all is well with the world. And yet closer examination reveals that even in these uplifting verses there is an undercurrent of anger and fear.

To order a copy of this book, please use the order form on page 151 or visit **brfonline.org.uk**.

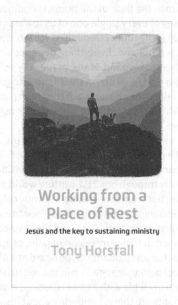

Working from a Place of Rest

Jesus and the key to sustaining ministry

Tony Horsfall

In striving to do our utmost for God, we can easily forget that there were many times when Jesus was willing to rest, to do nothing except wait for the Spirit's prompting, so that he demonstrated the vital principle of 'working from a place of rest'. In this new edition, Tony Horsfall reflects on the story of Jesus and the Samaritan woman to draw out practical guidance for sustainable Christian life and work.

Working from a Place of Rest
Jesus and the key to sustaining ministry
Tony Horsfall
978 1 80039 220 5 £8.99 publishing July 2023
brfonline.org.uk

To order

Online: brfonline.org.uk
Telephone: +44 (0)1865 319700
Mon–Fri 9.30–17.00

Delivery times within the UK are normally 15 working days. Prices are correct at the time of going to press but may change without prior notice.

Title	Price	Qty	Total
World Turned Upside Down	£12.99		
Working from a Place of Rest	£8.99		
Bible in Ten	£12.99		

POSTAGE AND PACKING CHARGES			
Order value	UK	Europe	Rest of world
Under £7.00	£2.00		
£7.00–£29.99	£3.00	Available on request	Available on request
£30.00 and over	FREE		

Total value of books	
Donation*	
Postage and packing	
Total for this order	

* Please complete and return the Gift Aid declaration on page 143.

Please complete in BLOCK CAPITALS

Title .... First name/initials .... Surname ....

Address ....

.... Postcode ....

Acc. No. .... Telephone ....

Email ....

Method of payment

❑ Cheque (made payable to BRF) ❑ MasterCard / Visa

Card no. ☐☐☐☐ ☐☐☐☐ ☐☐☐☐ ☐☐☐☐ ☐☐☐☐ ☐☐☐☐

Expires end ☐M☐M ☐Y☐Y Security code* ☐☐☐ *Last 3 digits on the reverse of the card

We will use your personal data to process this order. From time to time we may send you information about the work of BRF. Please contact us if you wish to discuss your mailing preferences **brf.org.uk/privacy**

Registered with
FUNDRAISING REGULATOR

Please return this form to:

BRF, 15 The Chambers, Vineyard, Abingdon OX14 3FE | **enquiries@brf.org.uk**

For terms and cancellation information, please visit **brfonline.org.uk/terms**.

BRF needs you!

If you're one of our regular *Guidelines* readers, you will know all about the benefits and blessings of regular Bible study and the value of serious daily notes to guide, inform and challenge you.

Here are some recent comments from *Guidelines* readers:

'… very thoughtful and spiritually helpful. [These notes] are speaking to the church as it is today, and therefore to Christians like us who live in today's world.'

'You have assembled an amazingly diverse group of people and their contributions are most certainly thoughtful.'

If you have similarly positive things to say about *Guidelines*, would you be willing to share your experience with others? Could you ask for a brief slot during church notices or write a short piece for your church magazine or website? Do you belong to groups, formal or informal, academic or professional, where you could share your experience of using *Guidelines* and encourage others to try them?

It doesn't need to be complicated: just answering these three questions in what you say or write will get your message across:

- How do *Guidelines* Bible study notes help you grow in knowledge and faith?
- Where, when and how do you use them?
- What would you say to people who haven't yet tried them?

We can supply further information if you need it and would love to hear about it if you do give a talk or write an article.

For more information:
- Email **enquiries@brf.org.uk**
- Telephone BRF on +44 (0)1865 319700 Mon–Fri 9.30–17.00
- Write to us at BRF, 15 The Chambers, Vineyard, Abingdon OX14 3FE

Enabling all ages to grow in faith

At BRF, we long for people of all ages to grow in faith and understanding of the Bible. That's what all our work as a charity is about.

- BRF's **Living Faith** ministry looks to see our founder Leslie Mannering's vision – to help people 'get a move on' spiritually – fulfilled in the 21st century. Our wide range of resources promotes Bible reading and prayer, our events bring people together to share this journey, and our Holy Habits initiative helps congregations grow in whole-life discipleship.

- We also want to make it easier for local churches to engage effectively in ministry and mission – by helping them bring new families into a growing relationship with God through **Messy Church** or by supporting churches as they nurture the spiritual life of older people through **Anna Chaplaincy**.

- Our **Parenting for Faith** team coaches parents and others to raise God-connected children and teens, and enables churches to fully support them.

Do you share our vision?

Though a significant proportion of BRF's funding is generated through our charitable activities, we are dependent on the generous support of individuals, churches and charitable trusts.

If you share our vision, would you help us to enable even more people of all ages to grow in faith? Your prayers and financial support are vital for the work that we do. You could:

- Support BRF's ministry with a regular donation;
- Support us with a one-off gift;
- Consider leaving a gift to BRF in your will (see page 154);
- Encourage your church to support BRF as part of your church's giving to home mission – perhaps focusing on a specific ministry or programme;
- Most important of all, support BRF with your prayers.

Donate at **brf.org.uk/donate** or use the form on pages 143–44.

Bringing people together

For where two or three gather in my name, there am I with them.
MATTHEW 18:20 (NIV)

After the events of the past few years, the privilege of being able to gather together has never felt more apparent. Whether it be for church services, concerts, sports matches, picnics or all manner of other activities, even the most introverted among us can experience the joy of being together with others.

Our ministries have always brought people together in the name of Jesus: Messy Churches bring the families of their communities under one roof; parents and church leaders meet together to take a Parenting for Faith course; Anna Chaplains bring companionship and support to older people experiencing loneliness. Our Living Faith resources also bring people together, a community of people reading the same Bible notes across the globe – not to mention events like the Festival of Prayer.

As always, BRF adapts to help even more people encounter Jesus, with more and more opportunities to meet in new ways: Messy Church Goes Wild taking their families outside, Messy Church and Parenting for Faith Facebook Live sessions, a community of podcast listeners, online Holy Habits courses and still more. It is a real privilege to be able to create spaces and communities where people can gather and thus be with Jesus.

We want to keep building on the work of the past 100 years, adapting and growing and finding even more glorious ways for people to grow in their faith as individuals and communities.

Our work would not be possible without kind donations from individuals, charitable trusts and gifts in wills. If you would like to support BRF's work now and in the future, you can become a Friend of BRF by making a monthly gift of £2 a month or more. We thank you for your friendship.

Find out more at **brf.org.uk/donate**.

Judith Moore
Fundraising development officer

Give. Pray. Get involved.
brf.org.uk

Please note our new subscription rates, current until 30 April 2024:

Individual subscriptions
covering 3 issues for under 5 copies, payable in advance
(including postage & packing):

	UK	Europe	Rest of world
Guidelines 1-year subscription	£19.05	£26.55	£30.45
Guidelines 3-year subscription (9 issues)	£54.45	N/A	N/A

Group subscriptions
covering 3 issues for 5 copies or more, sent to one UK address (post free):

Guidelines 1-year subscription	£14.85 per set of 3 issues p.a.

Please note that the annual billing period for group subscriptions runs from
1 May to 30 April.

Overseas group subscription rates
Available on request. Please email **enquiries@brf.org.uk**.

Copies may also be obtained from Christian bookshops:

Guidelines	£4.95 per copy

All our Bible reading notes can be ordered online
by visiting **brfonline.org.uk/subscriptions**

GUIDELINES

Guidelines is also available as
an app for Android, iPhone and iPad
brfonline.org.uk/apps

GUIDELINES INDIVIDUAL SUBSCRIPTION FORM

All our Bible reading notes can be ordered online by visiting
brfonline.org.uk/subscriptions

Title _____ First name/initials _____ Surname _____
Address _____

_____ Postcode _____

Telephone _____ Email _____

Please send *Guidelines* beginning with the September 2023 / January 2024 /
May 2024 issue (*delete as appropriate*):

(*please tick box*)

	UK	Europe	Rest of world
Guidelines 1-year subscription	☐ £19.05	☐ £26.55	☐ £30.45
Guidelines 3-year subscription	☐ £54.45	N/A	N/A

Optional donation to support the work of BRF £ _____

Total enclosed £ _____ (cheques should be made payable to 'BRF')

Please complete and return the Gift Aid declaration on page 143 to make your
donation even more valuable to us.

Please charge my MasterCard / Visa with £ _____

Card no. ☐☐☐☐ ☐☐☐☐ ☐☐☐☐ ☐☐☐☐

Expires end ☐M☐M ☐Y☐Y   Security code ☐☐☐   Last 3 digits on the reverse of the card

To set up a Direct Debit, please complete the Direct Debit instruction on page 159.

We will use your personal data to process this order. From time to time we may send you
information about the work of BRF. Please contact us if you wish to discuss your mailing
preferences **brf.org.uk/privacy**

Please return this form with the appropriate payment to:
BRF, 15 The Chambers, Vineyard, Abingdon OX14 3FE
For terms and cancellation information, please visit **brfonline.org.uk/terms**.

Bible Reading Fellowship is a charity (233280) and company limited by guarantee (301324),
registered in England and Wales

GL0223

GUIDELINES GIFT SUBSCRIPTION FORM

☐ I would like to give a gift subscription (please provide both names and addresses):

Title .... First name/initials .... Surname ....

Address ....

.... Postcode ....

Telephone .... Email ....

Gift subscription name ....

Gift subscription address ....

.... Postcode ....

Gift message (20 words max. or include your own gift card):

....

....

Please send *Guidelines* beginning with the September 2023 / January 2024 / May 2024 issue *(delete as appropriate)*:

(please tick box)

	UK	Europe	Rest of world
Guidelines 1-year subscription	☐ £19.05	☐ £26.55	☐ £30.45
Guidelines 3-year subscription	☐ £54.45	N/A	N/A

Optional donation to support the work of BRF £ ....

Total enclosed £ .... (cheques should be made payable to 'BRF')

Please complete and return the Gift Aid declaration on page 143 to make your donation even more valuable to us.

Please charge my MasterCard / Visa with £ ....

Card no.

Expires end | M | M | Y | Y | Security code | | | | Last 3 digits on the reverse of the card

To set up a Direct Debit, please complete the Direct Debit instruction on page 159.

We will use your personal data to process this order. From time to time we may send you information about the work of BRF. Please contact us if you wish to discuss your mailing preferences **brf.org.uk/privacy**

Please return this form with the appropriate payment to:
BRF, 15 The Chambers, Vineyard, Abingdon OX14 3FE
For terms and cancellation information, please visit **brfonline.org.uk/terms**.

Bible Reading Fellowship is a charity (233280) and company limited by guarantee (301324), registered in England and Wales

You can pay for your annual subscription to our Bible reading notes using Direct Debit. You need only give your bank details once, and the payment is made automatically every year until you cancel it. If you would like to pay by Direct Debit, please use the form opposite, entering your BRF account number under 'Reference number'.

You are fully covered by the Direct Debit Guarantee:

The Direct Debit Guarantee

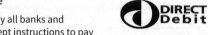

- This Guarantee is offered by all banks and building societies that accept instructions to pay Direct Debits.
- If there are any changes to the amount, date or frequency of your Direct Debit, Bible Reading Fellowship will notify you 10 working days in advance of your account being debited or as otherwise agreed. If you request Bible Reading Fellowship to collect a payment, confirmation of the amount and date will be given to you at the time of the request.
- If an error is made in the payment of your Direct Debit, by Bible Reading Fellowship or your bank or building society, you are entitled to a full and immediate refund of the amount paid from your bank or building society.
- If you receive a refund you are not entitled to, you must pay it back when Bible Reading Fellowship asks you to.
- You can cancel a Direct Debit at any time by simply contacting your bank or building society. Written confirmation may be required. Please also notify us.

GL0223

Instruction to your bank or building society to pay by Direct Debit

Please fill in the whole form using a ballpoint pen and return with order form to:
BRF, 15 The Chambers, Vineyard, Abingdon OX14 3FE

Service User Number: | 5 | 5 | 8 | 2 | 2 | 9 |

Name and full postal address of your bank or building society

To: The Manager	Bank/Building Society
Address	
	Postcode

Name(s) of account holder(s)

Branch sort code

| | | – | | | – | | |

Bank/Building Society account number

| | | | | | | | |

Reference number

| | | | | | | |

Instruction to your Bank/Building Society

Please pay Bible Reading Fellowship Direct Debits from the account detailed in this instruction, subject to the safeguards assured by the Direct Debit Guarantee. I understand that this instruction may remain with Bible Reading Fellowship and, if so, details will be passed electronically to my bank/building society.

Signature(s)

and Building Societies may not accept Direct Debit instructions for some
ccount.